D0359155

AMERICA AND THE BRITISH LEFT

AMERICA AND THE BRITISH LEFT

FROM BRIGHT TO BEVAN

BY

HENRY PELLING

FELLOW OF THE QUEEN'S COLLEGE, OXFORD

LONDON
ADAM AND CHARLES BLACK

FIRST PUBLISHED 1956
A. AND C. BLACK LTD.
4, 5 AND 6 SOHO SQUARE LONDON W.I

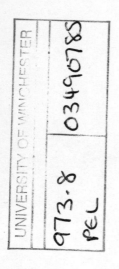

MADE IN GREAT BRITAIN
PRINTED BY UNWIN BROTHERS LTD., WOKING AND LONDON

TO MY FRIENDS
ERICA AND ALAN PIFER
WITH AFFECTION

CONTENTS

PREFACE

This book is an attempt to illustrate the attitude to the United States of the members of the British Left—first Liberal and Radical, later also Socialist—in the period since the American Civil War and up to the present day. It consists of a series of studies of particular controversies in British politics which throw light on the contemporary view of America. The studies do not attempt to assess the "impact" of America in relation to other factors in British politics: and the reader should beware of overestimating the importance of that influence from the selective evidence here presented. Nevertheless, it will be apparent to the reader that those textbooks of recent history which deal with Anglo-American relations only in terms of diplomatic contacts are ignoring a substantial and significant section of the history of Atlantic civilization.

Whatever merits these essays may possess must very largely be ascribed to the wealth of assistance which I received in the course of their preparation. Whatever faults they contain must be attributed to my failure to make the best use of this assistance. I am especially indebted to the scholars of the University of Wisconsin who made my stay in their midst in 1953–4 so pleasant and so stimulating an experience. To Professor Merle Curti I owe my introduction to that university; in my venture into his own chosen field of intellectual history, I was able to rely on his unfailing generosity and rich resources of knowledge. Professors Selig Perlman and Edwin Young extended to me much help in the sphere of American labour history, in which the "Wisconsin School" has long held the lead. Others, notably Professors Leon Epstein and Howard K. Beale, repeatedly went out of their way to assist my efforts to comprehend the American present and past.

In my search for primary sources in the United States I owe much to scholars working on kindred subjects: I must name Mr. R. V. Clements, Dr. Clifton Yearley, Miss Fola LaFollette, Professor Howard H. Quint and Professor David A. Shannon. I am also indebted to Mr. Marcus Cunliffe of Manchester University and to Dr. Frank Friedel, the present Harmsworth Professor at Oxford, for undertaking the labour of reading my entire manuscript and for making many valuable suggestions for its improvement. Mr. Frank Bealey, Miss Maureen Bullen, Professor Howard H. Quint, Mr. G. A. Shepperson, Mr. David Widdicombe and Professor C. Vann Woodward have at my request performed a similar service for individual chapters.

I am very grateful to the following for permission to consult and to quote from documents: the President of the American Federation of Labor, for A.F.L. headquarter correspondence files and for the papers of Samuel Gompers; Mrs. Vivian H. Seymer and Mrs. Charles Wrinch, for the papers of their father, W. H. Buckler; the Principal of Ruskin College, Oxford, for Dennis Hird's "Ruskin College Scrapbooks"; the Curator, Edward M. House Collection, Yale University Library, for the House Collection; Miss M. G. Wallas, for the papers of her father, Graham Wallas; the Passfield Trustees, for the papers of Sidney and Beatrice Webb; Mrs. Woodrow Wilson, for the papers of President Wilson.

Chapter V of this book has previously been published as an article in the *Economic History Review*, and I am grateful to the editor of that journal for permission to reprint it with only slight alterations.

I record also my appreciation of the patient co-operation afforded me by the staffs of the Bishopsgate Institute, the Bodleian Library, the British Library of Political and Economic Science, the British Museum, the Library of Congress, the Library of the Department of Labor (Washington, D.C.), the New York Public Library, Nuffield College Library, the Stevens Institute of Technology, the Wisconsin State Historical Library, and the Libraries of the following universities: University of California (Los Angeles), Catholic University of America (Washington, D.C.), Columbia, Duke, Harvard, Princeton, Wisconsin, Yale.

Finally, my work on this subject could not have been attempted without the award of a Fellowship by the Government of the United States under the Smith-Mundt Act; and I am obliged to the Provost and Fellows of The Queen's College for allowing me a year's leave of absence in order to take advantage of the award.

OXFORD, *December* 1955   HENRY PELLING

AMERICA AND THE BRITISH LEFT

CHAPTER I

INTRODUCTION

BRITISH Radicalism was born in the later eighteenth century, during the struggle of the American colonies for independence, and when the American question was in Burke's phrase being "beat backwards and forwards, as the tennis-ball of faction." From the first, the Radicals identified themselves with the American cause: for them it was a question of principle and not, as for many of the Whigs, a matter of expediency, to resist the claims of the Crown and the unreformed Parliament. Major Cartwright wrote a pamphlet in 1775 on *American Independence, The Interest and Glory of Great Britain*, and this set the pattern of enthusiasm for what Richard Price ten years later called "the fairest experiment ever tried in human affairs."[1]

How could it have been otherwise? Radicalism was essentially a protest movement against the most conservative elements of British society, the Crown and the aristocracy which between them controlled the political system. The Radicals found their ideal across the Atlantic because, as Tom Paine said, "the system of Government purely representative, unmixed with anything of hereditary nonsense, began in America."[2] If the early stages of the French Revolution for a time provided an alternative focus of interest, its later course of terror, reaction and Bonapartism left the field free again for admiration of the United States; and the material prosperity of America, combined with the cheapness of their governmental expenditure, did not pass unnoticed by the British Radicals.

Radicalism was at a discount in Britain in the period of the Napoleonic Wars, owing to the patriotic reaction of the time: it did not again gather strength until the 1820's, by which time the Jacksonian movement had developed in the United States. Bentham, Cobbett, and the rising working-class Radicals of

[1] Richard Price, *Observations on the Importance of the American Revolution, and the Means of Making it a Benefit to the World* (London, 1785), p. 85.
[2] Thomas Paine, *Letter to Mr. Henry Dundas* (London, 1792), p. 9.

Britain welcomed the transition to universal suffrage across the Atlantic, and only a tiny minority of Socialistic writers went so far as to suggest that the individual might suffer severely in America from "the errors of society."[1] The bulk of Chartist opinion was to the effect that the American working man was a good deal better off than his British counterpart; and Lovett and his friends of the National Association were not acting untypically when in 1846, in the midst of the Oregon dispute, they hailed the Republic as "a beacon to cheer and animate the friends of human rights and equal laws."[2] There was much to appeal to all types of British Radical: Benthamites approved of the liberal constitutions of the states; dissenters and freethinkers acclaimed the absence of a religious establishment; land reformers noted with favour the abundance of cheap and undeveloped land; working men found in America a paradise of high wages and social equality. By the 1840's, improvements in shipping combined with the good opinions of America now current among the British working class to stimulate the resumption of large-scale emigration.

*   *   *

This favourable view of America among Radicals and throughout the ranks of labour is the more remarkable when contrasted with the general antipathy of the British upper class, whose pride had been hurt by the loss of the colonies in the War of Independence. The growth of democracy, which heightened Radical enthusiasm, served at the same time to increase the fears of conservatives, and gave them a special motive for criticizing the Republic of the West, which was indeed the only state of any size in which democratic institutions existed. Switzerland was too small and too geographically peculiar to be taken into account; the British Australian colonies, though large enough geographically, were too poor and too sparsely populated to provide much of an example; the French attempts at democratic government had all ended abruptly and ingloriously in a *coup d'état*.

[1] *Economist*, 2 Feb. 1821.
[2] R. H. Tawney (ed.), *Life and Struggles of William Lovett* (London, 1920), ii, 321. For numerous quotations from the British Radical press further illustrating this attitude, see G. D. Lillibridge, *Beacon of Freedom* (Philadelphia, 1954).

British opponents of universal suffrage believed that De Tocqueville's *Democracy in America* provided all the evidence that they needed to justify their fears. In fact, De Tocqueville had found much to praise in American institutions: but the prejudiced reader, by selective quotation, could readily build up an indictment from his pages. As early as 1837 Sir Robert Peel, seeking arguments to support his newly-defined Conservatism, had seized upon De Tocqueville's description of the dangers of a "tyranny of the majority."[1] This tyranny, according to the visiting French aristocrat, had resulted in a uniform vulgarity of manners and mediocrity among the American people, and especially in their political representatives. The English reading public could readily find confirmatory evidence in the scathing remarks of Mrs. Trollope's *Domestic Manners of the Americans*, and in the bitter satire of Dickens's *Martin Chuzzlewit*. Indeed, criticism of American manners was a favourite topic of contemporary literary comment. Carlyle thought that the supreme achievement of the American people was to have "begotten, with a rapidity beyond recorded example, Eighteen Millions of the greatest bores ever seen in this world before";[2] Ruskin spoke of the transatlantic "lust of wealth, and trust in it; vulgar faith in magnitude and multitude, instead of nobleness; . . . perpetual self-contemplation issuing in passionate vanity; total ignorance of the finer and higher arts. . . .";[3] and Matthew Arnold urged the necessity of finding some way to prevent the English people from becoming "Americanized."[4]

The identification of "Americanizing" with "democratizing" was widespread: for the upper-class Conservative it meant "vulgarizing" as well. "I think . . . we are fast merging into Democracy and Americanism," wrote Lady Palmerston to Monckton Milnes in 1858: "Sir Hamilton Seymour teaches his children to speak thro' their noses as that is what he thinks they

---

[1] *Correct Report of Sir Robert Peel's Speeches at Glasgow* (London, 1837), pp. 82–6.

[2] T. Carlyle, *Latter-Day Pamphlets* (London, 1850), p. 21.

[3] J. Ruskin, in *Munera Pulveris* (1863); reprinted in *Works*, ii (Orpington, Kent, 1872), pp. 130 f.

[4] M. Arnold, Preface to *Popular Education in France* (1861); reprinted in *Mixed Essays* (London, 1879), p. 23.

must all come to"; [1] and in November 1866, at the height of the reform agitation, G. S. Venables, the leader-writer of *The Times* and the *Saturday Review*, wrote to Milnes in a state of depression and alarm: "Perhaps an American England may produce a higher average of happiness than the existing system, but it would not be a country for a gentleman, and I for one would be quite a stranger in it." [2]

*   *   *

The purpose of the present study is to show how the fund of Radical goodwill for America and its institutions, which made such a contrast with the prejudices of the "educated" classes in the middle of the nineteenth century, was gradually dissipated in the succeeding decades, until by the middle of the twentieth century the bulk of so-called "anti-American" feeling was to be found among the adherents of the Left in British politics. This process was not, of course, unique to Britain: the Radicals of other countries to some extent at least came under the same spell of enthusiasm for America, and went through the same stages of disillusionment. [3] But the people of Britain, who spoke the same language as the Americans, who regarded them as their kin, and who had the most frequent diplomatic and commerical contacts with them, were naturally most influenced by the course of thought and events in the United States. [4] Objective factors inevitably bulk large in accounting for the change of attitude: one may mention the enormous growth of American industry after the Civil War, which put an end to the Jeffersonian ideal of a commonwealth based on rural simplicity; the increasing participation of the United States in world politics, which deprived its statesmen of the reputation for disinterested diplomacy derived from the policy of isolation; and the increasing restrictions placed

[1] J. Pope-Hennessy, *Monckton Milnes: The Flight of Youth* (London, 1951), p. 36.

[2] T. Wemyss Reid, *Life of Lord Houghton* (London, 1890), i, 158 f.

[3] See, e.g., D. Hecht, *Russian Radicals Look to America* (Cambridge, Mass., 1947); H. Koht, *The American Spirit in Europe* (Philadelphia, 1949), which has a useful short bibliography.

[4] See F. Thistlethwaite, *The Great Experiment* (Cambridge, England, 1955); G. D. Lillibridge, *op. cit.*

upon immigration, which signified the closing of the "golden door" mentioned in the inscription on the Statue of Liberty. But in addition, subjective factors were of great importance: the growth of Socialist influences among the Radicals and in the Labour movement gave rise to suspicion of any country whose economy was founded on economic laissez-faire, however democratic its constitutional arrangements.

The chapters that follow attempt to provide illustrations of this changing attitude of the British Left—snapshots of a long, complicated, and continuous transformation of ideas—as it was revealed at different times in various important political controversies. The snapshots are not all taken from the same angle: the actors change, and the debate readily moves from the House of Commons and the great national newspapers and periodicals to Radical meetings, Socialist tracts, and trade union journals. To treat of the subject in its entirety would be impossible in a work of limited length; and many interesting, if subordinate, topics have been left unexplored.

The first study (Chapter II), which deals with the debate on Parliamentary reform in 1865–7, shows the extreme Radicals, both in Parliament and outside, acting as apologists for American democracy, in the face of strong Conservative hostility to the institutions of the Republic: it was the pattern of attitudes which had existed since the colonies became independent, but which was destined slowly to dissolve. After another decade the criticism of America still came from the Conservatives, and the defence from the Radicals: but Chapter III, dealing with the years 1877–9, finds the Radicals in some embarrassment when their new extraparliamentary political organization, the National Liberal Federation, was identified with the corruption of American machine politics. We see also some of the labour leaders beginning to chafe at the leadership of the middle-class Radicals.

By the later eighteen-eighties, the subject of Chapter IV, the tendency of change is unmistakable: a new economic Radicalism made its appearance, and also the beginnings of a Socialist movement. These new political forces were markedly critical of American institutions, and none the less so because Conservative thought now found a source of comfort in the political stability of

B

the Republic. Chapter V describes the further development of British Socialism, and shows how it formed an alliance with the trade union leadership at a time when the latter had come to have grave fears about the growth of industrial monopoly in the United States. No comparable alliance of left-wing forces was effected in America itself: and Chapters VI and VII, dealing with the relations of the labour movements of the two countries before and during the First World War, depict some of the consequences of this fact—the extremism of many American Socialists, and their influence in stimulating the British "Labour Unrest"; and, later, the conservatism of the American Labour leadership and its failure to appreciate the policy of the Labour Party during the war.

The last two chapters, dealing respectively with the nineteen-thirties and the period since the Second World War, complete the reversal of the old Radical attitude to America, with Socialist ideas influencing British labour into strong suspicions of American capitalism. Only the very much more pragmatic view of the British trade union leadership prevented these suspicions from seriously affecting Anglo-American relations in the years after the war when the Labour Party was in power.

The historical perspective provided by these studies inevitably suggests that dangerous distortion of the facts is likely to take place among those who commit themselves most fully to an *a priori* view of politics. Socialists of the mid-twentieth century seem to be often as blind to the merits of American society as Radicals of the mid-nineteenth century were blind to its faults. Although transatlantic institutions have undergone profound changes in the intervening period, many of the characteristics which were once admired, and rightly admired, by British reformers are ignored by their present-day successors. There are, however, some indications, discussed in the concluding pages, of a further change of attitude: provided that recent trends are not thrown out of balance by unforeseeable world events, more realistic assessments of American society, it is suggested, may now be hoped for from British left-wing thinkers and political leaders.

CHAPTER II

AMERICA AND THE BRITISH REFORM STRUGGLE, 1865-7

THE story of the crisis in Anglo-American relations caused by the American Civil War is an oft-told tale, but the pattern of events is now known to be not as simple as was once believed.[1] Considerations of national interest or of immediate political expediency often ran counter to the sympathies that individuals might feel for one side or the other; nor was it clear at the outset even where these sympathies would lie. It might be supposed that the Liberals and Radicals, with their inclination in favour of all features of the American polity except for its retention of slavery, would uniformly support the Northern cause, while the Conservatives and Whigs would find comfort in the hope of a victory for the Southern slave-owners, which would bring into existence a socially conservative state at the expense of the united democracy. In fact, however, we find Conservative leaders, for the sake of ultimate party advantage, restraining their more impetuous followers from too open an opposition to the Union cause; and many Liberals including Gladstone and Acton, and even for a time so notable a Radical spokesman as Richard Cobden, were led by their enthusiasm for free-trade policies and for the rights of small nations or sectional minorities to sympathize with the claims of the Confederates.[2] Even *Reynolds's Newspaper*, the well-known Radical weekly, at first denounced the Northern blockade for depriving the Lancashire cotton workers of their livelihood.[3]

[1] See E. D. Adams, *Great Britain and the American Civil War* (2 vols., London, 1925); D. Jordan and E. J. Pratt, *Europe and the American Civil War* (London, 1931); M. Beloff, "Great Britain and the American Civil War," *History*, xxxvii (1952), 40-2; Wilbur D. Jones, "The British Conservatives and the American Civil War," *American Historical Review*, lviii (1953), 527-43.

[2] C. Collyer, "Gladstone and the American Civil War," *Proceedings of the Leeds Philosophical Society*, vi (1951), 583-94; J. Morley, *Life of Richard Cobden* (London, 1881), ii, 372 f. For Acton's support of the Southern cause, based on approval of the States' Rights theory, see his letter to Robert E. Lee in 1866, quoted D. S. Freeman, *Robert E. Lee* (New York, 1935), iv, 516 f.

[3] "Better fight the Yankees than starve the operatives. . . . The American blockade must be broken."—Leader, *Reynolds's Newspaper*, 29 Sept. 1861.

On the Liberal and Radical side, however, a good deal of the confusion was due to doubt about the intentions of the Federal Government with respect to the slavery issue. After Lincoln's Emancipation Proclamation of September 1862 had clarified the administration's policy, there was a general hardening of Liberal, Radical and working-class opinion in favour of the Union. Abolitionism was a popular cause in Britain: it was significant that *Uncle Tom's Cabin* had been a prodigious best-seller throughout the country.[1] The Lancashire cotton workers, who suffered most directly from the blockade, now enthusiastically declared their support for Lincoln,[2] and aroused the admiration of Gladstone for those "little tutored, but yet reflective minds" whose political prescience exceeded his own.[3]

In the end, therefore, the American war helped to develop a certain bond of unity between moderate Liberals, Radicals, and working men. This unity, useful as it was to Lincoln and his cabinet in the later part of the war, also had considerable importance for the future development of British politics. It helped powerfully to solidify the loose alliance of forces that was coming to be recognized as "the Liberal Party," and gave it the necessary impetus to proceed to a bold measure of Parliamentary reform. This was demonstrated in the 1865 elections, a feature of which was the success of Radicals such as John Stuart Mill, Thomas Hughes and Henry Fawcett, who had all been prominent in the advocacy of the Northern cause. Charles Francis Adams, the American minister in London, noticed the quickening demand for reform and reported home:

It is impossible not to perceive traces of the influence of our institutions upon all these changes. . . . The progress of the Liberal cause, not in England alone, but all over the world, is in a measure, in our hands.[4]

[1] Forty editions (not re-issues) within twelve months of publication (Apr. 1852. and a million and a half copies all told for Britain and the British colonies. C) Gohdes, *American Literature in Nineteenth Century England* (New York, 1944), p. 29.

[2] Prof. F. L. Owsley has argued, in his *King Cotton Diplomacy* (Chicago, 1931), ch. vi, that there was little popular enthusiasm for the North in Lancashire; but the evidence he cites is almost exclusively from the files of the Anglo-Confederate journal the *Index* and from the papers of Confederate agents.

[3] *Parliamentary Debates*, 3rd. ser., clxxxiii, 148 (27 Apr. 1866).

[4] *Papers Relating to Foreign Affairs*, First Session, 39th Congress, Part 1 (Washington D.C., 1866), p. 417.

It is true that complete unity among the reforming forces was not obtained. The extra-parliamentary agitation was carried on by a number of bodies which were more radical in aim than all save a tiny minority of M.P.s. The National Reform Union, formed in 1864 by John Bright and others to work for household suffrage and the ballot, constituted the right wing of a movement which also included the Reform League and the London Working Men's Association. The Reform League was founded in 1865 with the support of trade union leaders such as Odger and Applegarth, and its object was universal suffrage. The London Working Men's Association was run with a similar object but a separate organization: it was founded in 1866 by George Potter, who controlled the London labour weekly the *Beehive*. Potter was at odds with the trade union "Junta," to which Odger and Applegarth belonged. Substantially, however, there was much common ground between the three bodies, and the course of events enabled them to co-operate successfully.[1]

The franchise measure which Gladstone's government introduced in March 1866 was defeated in the Commons by a revolt of a Whig section of the Liberals, the Adullamites as they were nicknamed by John Bright. The Adullamites were led by Edward Horsman and Robert Lowe, and the debates of April and May were signalized by the latter's brilliant attack on the bill. In June the Liberal Government fell; and this was immediately followed by strong action on the part of the reform societies. In July occurred the famous Reform League meeting in Hyde Park, when the railings were knocked down; and other large demonstrations, in which the trade unions collaborated, were held in many cities and towns. The pressure continued throughout the winter and the spring of 1867, until in May the Conservative government accepted the principle of household suffrage in their own reform bill. With this "Conservative Surrender" (as Lord

---

[1] For an account of labour's part in the reform agitation, see F. E. Gillespie, *Labor and Politics in England, 1850-67* (Durham, N.C., 1927). George Howell's unpublished "Autobiography" (in the Bishopsgate Institute, London) contains a valuable account of the history of the Reform League. Howell, who was the League's secretary, mentions that support for the North "for a long time was regarded as a test of radicalism in English politics."

Cranborne called it)[1] the struggle was over, and in August the bill which enfranchised the bulk of the urban working class received the Royal assent.

*   *   *

Although this was purely an issue of British internal politics, America figured prominently throughout the controversy, and in the mouths of partisans on both sides was virtually a synonym for democracy. The Civil War problems of blockade rights, of British maritime interests, of free trade and of the supplies of cotton for the Lancashire mills, had largely lost their relevance, or had become subordinate to the main debate on the merits and defects of a democratic system. Bright and the other Radicals who wanted a considerable extension of the franchise found a favourable example of their aims in America; while those who were against any change in the constitution regarded America as an object-lesson of the dangers of democracy. It is surprising how rarely attempts were made to point out the special peculiarities of the American constitution, and the pitfalls of making direct comparisons between the two countries. American institutions, it is true, were little studied in Britain: the young James Bryce had not yet turned his mind in the direction that was to lead, more than twenty years later, to the *American Commonwealth*; and Bagehot's *English Constitution*, which drew a contrast between the British system and the American to the considerable disadvantage of the latter, was not published in book form until 1867, the year of decision on the reform issue.[2] In the course of the Commons debates Sir Edward Bulwer Lytton, the novelist, who sat as a Conservative M.P. for some years before becoming Lord Lytton, was one of the very few speakers to argue that the division of powers in the American constitution severely limited the effects of universal suffrage:

The wise safeguard of America against her popular suffrage is the scantiness of the powers she leaves to her House of Representatives. I

[1] *Quarterly Review*, cxxiii, 533–65 (Oct. 1867). Cranborne later became the Marquis of Salisbury and was three times Prime Minister as leader of the Conservative Party.

[2] It was, however, serialized in the *Fortnightly Review* in 1865–7.

dare say you might grant not only the £7 franchise, but even universal suffrage in this country, with safety as to foreign affairs, with safety as to making and unmaking Cabinets, and with safety to everything except genuine freedom, if you then left the House of Commons as little influence, power, weight and authority as are left to the Representative Chambers of America and France.[1]

To lump together the French legislature of the Second Empire and the American House of Representatives was, no doubt, unfair to the latter: but the main point was sound. Charles Adderley, who was Under-secretary for the Colonies in the Conservative Government of 1866–8, argued along similar lines in a pamphlet of 1865. If the English constitution were "democratized," he wrote, "the result would be far more democratic than anything existing under the constitution of the United States. Theirs would be a limited and balanced democracy, compared with ours."[2]

It was not uncommon, however, for speakers and writers to point out that America was specially favoured by geographical conditions. Samuel Laing, an Adullamite, argued that the Americans could risk democratic control of their foreign policy, for they had no powerful neighbours, and did not need the diplomatic qualities that were essential for Britain's complicated foreign relations.[3] But there was another advantage that the people of America possessed, which came in for more frequent mention. This was the possession of large tracts of free or cheap land, which Robert Lowe maintained was "a resource which removes and carries off all the peccant political humours of the body politic."[4] This anticipation of the safety-valve theory—actually an old theme in British discussions of American social development[5]— was exploited in the fullest way by the Parliamentary opponents of reform. Thus Disraeli, who had spoken of America at the end of the Civil War as having scope for expansion comparable

[1] *Parl. Deb.*, 3rd. ser., clxxxii, 1249 (13 Apr. 1866).
[2] C. B. Adderley, *Europe Incapable of American Democracy* (London, 1867), p. 39. Cf. Bagehot on the American "splitting of sovereignty," *Fortnightly Review*, vi, 811 (1 Dec. 1866).
[3] *Parl. Deb.*, 3rd ser., clxxxii, 1319 (16 Apr. 1866).
[4] *Ibid.*, clxxviii, 1438 (3 May 1865).
[5] See the evidence quoted by G. D. Lillibridge, *Beacon of Freedom*, p. 93.

to that of England at the end of the Wars of the Roses,[1] went on a year later to draw a contrast between the possibilities of the two countries for democratic experiment. There was little danger, he argued, in giving democratic institutions to a people who had "behind them an illimitable region where the landless might become landowners"; but Britain was in no such position. For her, a democratic constitution would be "disastrous":

If a dominant multitude were to succeed in bringing the land of England into the condition of the land in America, they would after all get but a limited area, and that only after a long struggle, in the course of which the great elements of our civilization would disappear, and England, from being a first-rate Kingdom, would become a third-rate Republic.[2]

Robert Lowe summed up his own closely similar analysis in the same debate by saying "In America land acts as a sedative to political passion; in England it acts as an irritant."[3]

Nevertheless, many of the arguments that the reformers had to face were based on a direct comparison with the American experience. Echoes of De Tocqueville sounded constantly in the discussions. "The Americans," said The Times, "have discovered that manhood suffrage means tyranny of a more pressing and galling kind than any aristocratic class are accused of exercising here."[4] The 1866 Congressional elections showed how the minority was swamped in each state, so that none but Republicans were elected except in states with a Democratic majority, where none but Democrats were elected. Thus the American parties assumed a sectional character. This, according to The Times, was the 'tyranny of the majority" at work.[5] One of The Times' leader-writers, Leonard Courtney, strongly favoured Thomas Hare's much-debated scheme for proportional representation, which was

[1] Parl. Deb., 3rd ser., clxxviii, 1703 (8 May 1865).
[2] Ibid., clxxxiii, 103 f. (27 Apr. 1866).
[3] Ibid., clxxxii, 2114 (26 Apr. 1866). The argument is echoed in the anonymous pamphlets, The Rock Ahead (Edinburgh, 1867), p. 21, and Reform (London, 1867), p. 31.
[4] The Times, 7 Sept. 1866.
[5] Ibid., 3 Dec. 1866 and 19 Jan. 1867. The Radical victory in the 1866 midterm elections certainly reflected very little credit on democratic institutions: see Howard K. Beale, The Critical Year (New York, 1930).

an attempt to overcome this "tyranny."[1] The amendment of the Reform Bill to provide that voters should have only two votes in three-member constituencies was made under the influence of such arguments.

The evil result of democratic "tyranny" in practice in America, it appeared to many, was that the best people abstained from politics. A writer in the *Contemporary Review* declared: "We cannot read their newspapers, or look at the debates of their Congress, without feeling that it is not the best or the greatest of the Americans who influence the public mind."[2] Lowe, in one of his speeches in the Commons debates, reported a comment of Emerson to the same effect;[3] and John Stuart Mill, now a Radical M.P., was reminded by his political opponents that in *Representative Government* he has spoken of American politics as "a most valuable school, but . . . a school from which the ablest teachers are excluded."[4]

But mediocrity was not half the accusation. The absence of "the best and greatest" from American political life was assumed to have resulted in a degeneration of the whole standard of government. A symbol of the degeneration was the "caucus" system—the system of holding meetings of politicians, often in secret, in order to determine party policy or the nomination of candidates in advance of public assembly. The word "caucus" was still in common use in America, although for the purpose of nominating candidates it had long been superseded by the "convention." But neither "caucus" nor "convention" had

[1] G. P. Gooch, *Life of Lord Courtney* (London, 1920), p. 84; T. Hare, *Election of Representatives* (3rd ed., London, 1865). Hare quoted Calhoun's *Disquisition on Government* on the dangers of "the uncontrolled government of the numerical majority" (*op. cit.*, p. 4).

[2] *Contemporary Review*, iii, 437 (1866); cf. *Saturday Review*, xix, 332 (25 Mar. 1865).

[3] *Parl. Deb.*, 3rd ser., clxxxiii, 1632 (31 May 1866); cf. H. W. Cole, *The Middle Classes and the Borough Franchise* (London, 1866), p. 1 (note) and p. 44.

[4] Adderley, *Parl. Deb.*, 3rd ser., clxxxii, 1421 (16 Apr. 1866); Whiteside, *ibid.*, clxxxiii, 1866 (4 June, 1866); "An Old Whig" (Thomas Ballantyne), *Americanization: a Letter to J. S. Mill, Esq., M.P.* (London, 1866), pp. 6 f. Mill, however, had taken heart from the favourable aspect of culture in New England. He wrote to E. L. Godkin in 1865 that "Democracy has been no leveller there as to intellect and education, or respect for true personal superiority."— Hugh Elliott (ed.), *Letters of J. S. Mill* (London, 1910), ii, 35.

so far had any close parallel in British politics, where the control both of parties in the House and of elections in the constituencies had been more personal and less formal, as one would expect in a "deferential" society. The possibility of the development in Britain of more disciplined party organization along American lines seemed to threaten the freedom of Parliamentary discussion. "The dominant party in Congress," said Lowe, "settle their policy in caucus out of the House, and silence the dissentient minority in the House, by moving the previous question."[1] Lord Cranborne was equally concerned with the "danger of drifting into a system of nominating caucuses" for the selection of candidates for regular constituencies.[2] No doubt he had read Bagehot's definition of the Presidential nominating caucus as "a sort of representative meeting which sits voting and voting until they have cut out all the known men."[3]

It was obvious, of course, that the extension of the suffrage would lead to some changes in party organization both in and out of Parliament, and a loss of much of the old intimate connexional character of politics. But the threat of the introduction of the "caucus" system, imperfectly understood as it was in its American setting, carried with it for the British upper class much more than the implication that it was a piece of political machinery better adapted to the larger constituencies of a more democratic electorate. It bore also a strong taint of corruption—corruption which, as the Adullamite W. H. Gregory suggested, was in America not "retail" as in England, but "wholesale," and "extended from the constituency to the representative." Gregory maintained (contrary to his own personal experience, it must be said) that in Britain the representative, who might have to bribe his constituents to secure election, at least retained a degree of personal independence as a member of Parliament; in America this was not usually the case.[4] A *Times* leader-writer agreed with him in this distinction:

[1] R. Lowe, *Speeches and Letters on Reform* (London, 1867), preface, p. 18.

[2] *Parl. Deb.*, 3rd ser., clxxxvii, 1357 (30 May 1867).

[3] *Fortnightly Review*, iv, 270 (15 Mar. 1866).

[4] *Parl. Deb.*, 3rd ser., clxxxii, 1792–4 (20 Apr. 1866). In 1842 Gregory, then aged twenty-five, had been returned for Dublin at a cost of £9,000. He had however been "obliged to give pledges to the extreme Conservative and

In England the candidate is the victim of it [sc. corruption], in America the public administration. There the candidate for Congress promises places, instead of giving money out of his own or his generous partner's pocket.[1]

It was Lowe, however, who made the strongest charges against the members of Congress. Among them, he said, were

. . . traffickers in office, bankrupts, men who have lost their character and been driven from every respectable way of life, and who take up politics as a last resort.[2]

Under these circumstances of legislative degeneracy, there was naturally much to condemn in the actual measures of the administration and Congress. Lord Robert Montagu revived the memory of Lincoln's suspension of Habeas Corpus.[3] The adoption of protective tariffs was condemned by several speakers and writers.[4] Beresford Hope, Lord Cranborne's brother-in-law and a strong supporter of the South in the Civil War, even diagnosed the appearance of Socialism in America, and feared that it would spread to Britain.[5] Lowe was so obsessed with the American parallel that he foresaw the introduction to Britain of almost every other American institution—an elected second chamber, elected judges, even elected army officers.[6]

Finally, the suggestion was made that the real object of the reformers was a republican government on the American model. "Was it not probable," said Sir Thomas Bateson,

Orange party, which were inconsistent with his real convictions and by which he subsequently felt himself considerably hampered."—*Dictionary of National Biography*, s.v. "W. H. Gregory."

[1] *The Times*, 7 Sept. 1866.

[2] *Parl. Deb.*, 3rd ser., clxxxii, 2107 (26 Apr. 1866).

[3] *Ibid.*, 1285 (13 Apr. 1866). Montagu was the author of a curious pamphlet, *A Mirror in America* (London, 1861), bitterly critical of American democracy and the Northern cause, and sustained by many arguments from Cicero.

[4] Gregory, *Parl. Deb.*, 3rd ser., clxxviii, 1622-4 (8 May 1865); M. H. Marsh, who also condemned the Maine Liquor Law, *ibid.*, clxxxii, 61 (12 Mar. 1866); Laing, *ibid.*, 1318 (13 Apr. 1866); Lowe, *ibid.*, 2105 f. (26 Apr. 1866); Frederic Hill, *Parliamentary Reform* (London, 1865), p. 8; "A. N.," letter in *National Reformer*, 23 Sept. 1866.

[5] *Parl. Deb.*, 3rd ser., clxxxii, 1690 (19 Apr. 1866); cf. *The Times* leader, 22 May 1867.

[6] *Ibid.*, 2113 (26 Apr. 1866); clxxxviii, 1544-6 (15 July 1867).

... that when the Constitution of Old England had been Americanized that an attack upon the monarchy of this country would very soon follow?[1]

Disraeli's comment, already quoted, that "England, from being a first-rate Kingdom, would become a third-rate Republic," pointed to the same prospect.

The horror of the Conservatives and the conservative-minded Whigs at the subversion of traditional elements of the constitution and their fear of the dangers in entrusting power to an uneducated democracy, are best summed up by Edward Horsman, who shared with Lowe the leadership of the Adullamites. Horsman deplored the possibility that

... the old tree of English liberty which had been the slow growth of ages and the admiration of nations should be transformed into the brazen image of ignorance and intolerance which the worshippers of Trans-Atlantic equality wanted to set up.[2]

★   ★   ★

These, then, were the charges against American democracy. How were they answered by the supporters of reform? Unity on the slavery issue in the later stages of the Civil War did not mean unity of enthusiasm afterwards for all the institutions of the United States. The various components of the reforming coalition each spoke with a different voice. First of all there were the moderate Liberals—in fact the main bulk of the Parliamentary Liberal Party under Gladstone—who while convinced of the need for some reform had no particular love for democracy, still less democracy on the American pattern. Secondly, there were the Parliamentary Radicals, the most prominent of whom was Bright, who like Turnbull in Anthony Trollope's *Phineas Finn* had "an almost idolatrous admiration for all political movements in America."[3] Thirdly, there was a group of intellectual Radicals outside the House, most of whom, while convinced of the desirability of achieving democracy, nevertheless conceded that all was

[1] *Parl. Deb.*, 3rd ser., clxxxiii, 1857 (4 June 1866).
[2] *Ibid.*, clxxxii, 98 f. (12 Mar. 1866).
[3] Anthony Trollope, *Phineas Finn* (World's Classics ed., 1937), i, 199. *Phineas Finn* was first published serially in 1867-9.

not well in the transatlantic model. And finally, there were the working-class Radicals, who had no foothold in Parliament, but a vocal press, many extra-Parliamentary orators, and an enthusiasm for America not excelled by that of Bright. Such a division of the supporters of reform is necessarily arbitrary, but is not without value in attempting an analysis of the arguments that were used.

The moderate Liberals endeavoured to escape from the direct parallel between England and America that their opponents drew. Goschen, for instance, who was prominent in City finance, sought to allay Beresford Hope's fears about Socialism spreading to Britain from the new countries. "In England," he said, "labour is dependent on capital, but in Australia and America, capital is dependent on labour."[1] Stansfield made a similar but more general point by stressing the traditional character of British life:

You must recollect that politics are, after all, only part of the life of a nation, that social conditions govern their possibilities, and you know that in this country you could not, if you would, Americanize or colonialize our institutions.[2]

C. P. Villiers, another moderate, in denying the validity of the American parallel, went back to 1832 to show how the same arguments from America had been brought up against the First Reform Bill.[3] The concern of this large group of Liberal opinion to avoid the comparison with America was best shown by Gladstone himself, in his rebuttal of Disraeli's attempt to impute "American principles" to the Liberal franchise proposals. Gladstone rebuked the Conservatives for speaking of "Americanizing the institutions of the country"—a tactic which, he suggested, would produce the reverse of what they intended, for it would magnify the influence of Bright.[4]

Bright's enthusiasm for the United States, fanned as it had been over the years of struggle for the Northern cause in the Civil War, was almost as strongly evident in his Commons speeches as in his popular orations. A Conservative M.P. complained that Bright never opened his mouth in Parliament without mentioning the

[1] *Parl. Deb.*, 3rd ser., clxxxii, 1966 (23 Apr. 1866).
[2] *Ibid.*, clxxviii, 1673 (8 May 1865). Cf. Butler-Johnstone (Independent Conservative) in supporting Disraeli's bill, *ibid.*, clxxxvi, 574 (26 Mar. 1867).
[3] *Ibid.*, clxxxii, 171 f. (13 Mar. 1866).
[4] *Ibid.*, clxxxiii, 119 (27 Apr. 1866).

United States.[1] He had summed up the advantages of the American polity in these words: "A free church, a free school, free land, a free vote, and a free career for the child of the humblest born in the land."[2] Nor did he find anything to criticize in the events of the war and the immediate Reconstruction period. He told his Birmingham constituents in 1866:

There you find a people exhibiting all the virtues which belong to the greatest nations on the face of the earth; there you find a people passing through a great war and a great revolution with a conduct and success, with a generosity and a magnanimity which have attracted and aroused the admiration of the world.[3]

Bright and his Radical colleagues pointed to the continued flow of migrants from Britain to the United States, to show that the working class at least found conditions to be better over there. The artisans, they argued, would continue to emigrate in large numbers until they lost the sense of estrangement in their own country, which was created by their disqualification from the suffrage. This point was made in the House by Thomas Hughes, W. E. Forster, and Henry Fawcett as well as by Bright himself.[4] Bright went so far as to compare the lot of the voteless British working man with that of the American negro before the Civil War.[5] But the Radicals made little attempt to deal in detail with the criticisms of American institutions in which some of their opponents indulged. If they did, they might find themselves on weak ground. A remark by W. E. Baxter—who undoubtedly knew better—that "there was nothing like bribery in American elections" drew cries of dissent from other Members, and a similar statement by Bright also occasioned immediate opposition.[6]

[1] Whiteside, *Parl. Deb.*, 3rd ser., clxxxii, 1908 (23 Apr. 1866).

[2] J. E. Thorold Rogers (ed.), *Speeches by John Bright, M.P.* (London, 1869), i, 223.

[3] *The Times*, 28 Aug. 1866.

[4] Hughes, *Parl. Deb.*, 3rd ser., clxxxii, 1709 (19 Apr. 1866); Forster, *ibid.*, clxxviii, 1643 (8 May 1865); Fawcett, *ibid.*, clxxxii, 208 (13 Apr. 1866); Bright, *ibid.*, 224 (13 Apr. 1866).

[5] *Ibid.*, 1900 f. (23 Apr. 1866). Cf. his letter read to a meeting on Primrose Hill (*The Times*, 23 May 1866).

[6] Baxter, *Parl. Deb.*, 3rd ser., clxxxii, 1235 (13 Apr. 1866); Bright, *ibid.*, clxxxiii, 1340 (28 May 1866). Baxter gave an account of American political corruption in his *America and the Americans* (London, 1855), pp. 57–60.

Forster was more effective in drawing attention to the advantages of the American educational system, which was a more obviously favourable feature of transatlantic life. "We want to have Old England as well taught as New England," he said.[1] Even weightier was John Stuart Mill's contention that De Tocqueville's views had been misinterpreted:

Let me refer hon. gentlemen to Tocqueville, who is so continually quoted when he says anything uncomplimentary to democracy, that those who have not read him might mistake him for an enemy of it, instead of its discriminating but sincere friend. Tocqueville says that, though the American legislatures are perpetually making mistakes, they are perpetually correcting them too; and that the evil, such as it is, is far outweighed by the salutary effects of the general tendency of their legislation, which is maintained, in a degree unknown elsewhere, in the direction of the interest of the people.[2]

There remained, however, much in the criticism of America that the little band of Parliamentary Radicals had not adequately dealt with. For a full examination of the charges against American democracy we must turn away from the rhetoric of the Parliamentarians, and examine the more reflective observations of our third group. Early in 1867 there was published a volume entitled *Essays on Reform*, which was written in collaboration by a number of younger Radicals, many of whom were university dons, and some of whom, notably Goldwin Smith, A. V. Dicey, James Bryce and Leslie Stephen, were to become distinguished men of letters. The constant references to the United States throughout the essays form the most striking feature of the book. Most of the essayists took a cautiously optimistic view of democracy. G. C. Brodrick, in the first essay, which was a reply to Lowe's speeches, argued as Mill had done, that De Tocqueville, on whom Lowe had leant so much, was favourably impressed by many features of American life. R. H. Hutton, who was joint editor of the *Spectator*, suggested, on the basis of the experience of the Civil War period, that the British working class had more understanding of the problems of other nations than had the other classes in the community: consequently its leaders were as well fitted to

---

[1] *Parl. Deb.*, 3rd ser., clxxxii, 1394 (16 Apr. 1866).
[2] *Ibid.*, 1261 f. (13 Apr. 1866).

supervise the nation's foreign policy.[1] Dicey maintained that the cause of the Civil War in America was not democracy but the federal system, and praised the Yankee artisans and farmers, as against the merchants of New York, for saving the Union. Lord Houghton, the former Monckton Milnes now raised to the peerage, conceded that a democratic government might make mistakes like the introduction of a protective system, but European autocracies were capable of similar errors. "Evils of this nature," he added dryly, "are incidental to the frailty of human nature and the imperfection of human knowledge."[2] Another contributor, A. O. Rutson, a Fellow of Magdalen College, Oxford, excused the faults of American politics by pointing to the special problems involved in educating and civilizing the "immigrant multitude."[3]

Two of the essays dealt more fully and seriously with America than did the others. These were the contributions of Leslie Stephen and Goldwin Smith. Leslie Stephen had actively espoused the Northern cause in the Civil War, had visited America in 1863, and was the author of a vigorous pamphlet criticizing the editorial policy of The Times during the war.[4] His essay was entitled "On the Choice of Representatives by Popular Constituencies," and in it he considered the contention that American statesmen had declined in ability since the War of Independence, and were now, owing to the influence of "the two idols, money and the mob," debased by corruption and demagogy.[5] Stephen accepted the charge as being largely true, and merely pleaded in mitigation, first, that American statesmanship never had been outstanding and so could hardly have declined, and, secondly, that the defect was due not so much to democracy as to the fact that America was a young country. He also maintained that the division of powers in the constitution made Congress resemble "a meeting of delegates from independent countries as much as a supreme legislature."[6] He shrewdly observed that "America is a country in

[1] This point was also made by Frederic Harrison in a somewhat similar volume of essays, Questions for a Reformed Parliament (London, 1867), p. 254.

[2] G. C. Brodrick et al., Essays on Reform (London, 1867), p. 66.

[3] Ibid., p. 284. Rutson was apparently the editor of the essays: see his letter to Bryce, 10 Dec. 1866, in Bryce Papers, Bodleian Library, Oxford.

[4] L. Stephen, The Times on the American War (London, 1865).

[5] Essays on Reform, p. 93.   [6] Ibid., p. 97.

which, owing to obvious circumstances, so little government of any kind is required, that the profession of governing sinks into a subordinate position."[1]

Stephen went on to accept, and to explain, the accusations of degeneracy in the American political system. New York political corruption, he showed, was caused by the difficulty of coping with the "overflowings of ignorance and pauperism" which had arrived from Europe.[2] "Log-rolling" in Congress was only a cruder form of the corruption that existed in British politics; the "caucus" was the American substitute for the aristocratic "influence" that held the British political parties together. The conclusion that Stephen came to was that

. . . the comparatively low standard of the political leaders in America depends upon many causes, some of which at least are totally inapplicable in England. Thus the actual insignificance in numbers of any highly educated class, the intrinsically small importance of political as compared with private life, the shifting and unstable condition of society, the constant influx of a poor foreign population, and the consequent absence of the system of hereditary party discipline, are all of them important causes, and all of them peculiar to America as distinguished from England.[3]

This was the summing-up of a thoughtful essay in which Stephen had conceded much of the opposition case about America, but was at pains to point out, as he himself put it in a letter to Oliver Wendell Holmes, Sr., "that an argument from the United States to England is necessarily unsafe, and often directly fallacious."[4]

Goldwin Smith had the task of writing an essay directly on "The Experience of the American Commonwealth." Smith was Regius Professor of Modern History at Oxford from 1858 to 1866, and two years later accepted a post at the new American university founded by Ezra Cornell. He had been as active as Stephen in support of the Union, and had also visited America in the course of the war. Smith could when he wished be as polemical as any of the Parliamentary Radicals, as may be seen from his address to the Oxford Reform League, in which he spoke of the 1864 Presidential election having passed off "like an English Sunday, with less

[1] *Essays on Reform*, p. 98.   [2] *Ibid.*, p. 99.   [3] *Ibid.*, p. 103.
[4] Letter dated 25 Mar. 1867, quoted in F. W. Maitland, *Life and Letters of Leslie Stephen* (London, 1906), pp. 194 f.

C

disturbance in the whole of the United States than there was at Mr. Lowe's first election for the little pocket borough of Calne."[1] It was in this address that he spoke of looking forward "to the day when a truly national Parliament will Americanize our pauperism and Americanize the yawning chasm btween rich and poor"; though he was careful to point out, in reply to alarmists like Beresford Hope, that communism could not prevail in a country like America "where every man may hope and does hope to rise to wealth."[2]

In *Essays on Reform*, however, Smith's tone was more moderate. He first sought to dispose of the Disraeli–Lowe argument about American land as a social safety-valve not available in Britain. "Wealth," he said, "is not only agricultural, but industrial; as many outlets and safety valves are supplied by our inventions and by the opening up of new lines of commerce as by the West." Besides, was it not possible to emigrate from England? "If America has an outlet to the West, England has outlets—her Colonies, and if she will only be kind to her own kin, in America itself."[3] Thus the frontier thesis later to be elaborated by the American historians almost exclusively in terms of their own continent was given by Goldwin Smith the broader, less purely American significance which it deserves.

Smith went on, much in the vein of Leslie Stephen, to mention some of the disadvantages which American democracy had to deal with, and some of the defects which it shared with aristocratic England. He did not concede quite as much, however, about the mediocrity of American statesmanship, although his order of merit was curious: "Many people think Lincoln, Grant, and Sherman eminent men, to say nothing of Mr. Stanton, whose super-human energy bore the burden of administering the war." But he was ready, too, with an explanation of mediocrity in a democratic state: as the general intelligence advances individual eminence declines, and "instead of individual greatness you have the greatness of a nation."[4]

[1] Goldwin Smith, *Address to Oxford Reform League* (Oxford, 1866), p. 13.

[2] *Ibid.*, pp. 14–16. Cf. J. E. Thorold Rogers in *Questions for a Reformed Parliament*, p. 275, where he uses this comparative peacefulness at the polling-booth as an argument for the ballot.

[3] *Essays on Reform*, p. 219.   [4] *Ibid.*, p. 236 f.

Essays on Reform was an interesting and not unsuccessful attempt to meet the charges made by Robert Lowe and the other critics of democracy. The essayists were not such blind enthusiasts for the American model that they could find no faults or failings in it. But they insisted that these faults and failings were either unimportant or inapplicable to Britain. On the whole, they were remarkably consistent in their attitude: but Robert Lowe, in an extended criticism of the volume in the *Quarterly Review*, was able to point to some contradictions and variations of view, although he raised no fresh arguments of substance.[1] By this time, in any case, the battle for reform was closing. The Derby–Disraeli government had accepted and carried through Parliament a measure which extended household suffrage to the boroughs: England had already taken the "Niagara leap" as Carlyle called it.[2] Disraeli, after assuring his Buckinghamshire constituents that he would not "remodel the institutions of the country upon any foreign type whatever, whether it be American or whether it be French,"[3] had proceeded to accept an extension of the franchise more radical than what Gladstone had proposed. Lowe therefore, feeling a little more charitable to his opponents after having been betrayed by his allies, concluded his review of *Essays on Reform* with the melancholy observation that "we owe some respect to the critics who alone have endeavoured to put into a permanent form the principles of the new order of things, and we take leave of them with the frank admission that though we cannot accept them for our teachers, they are undoubtedly our masters."

★   ★   ★

So far, nothing has been said about the attitude of the working-class leaders themselves to this debate about American democracy. They were none of them in Parliament itself; and they did not write volumes of essays. But they did have their own newspapers, and they held meetings and took part in vigorous extra-Parliamentary controversy. In these years, they did not have a separate political party of their own: most of them sympathized with the

---

[1] *Quarterly Review*, cxxiii, 244–77 (July 1867).
[2] "Shooting Niagara: and After?", *Macmillan's Magazine*, xvi (1867), 319 ff.
[3] *Annual Register*, 1866, p. 169.

aims of the Liberal Party, but formed a pressure group of the "labour interest" which exerted some influence in urging the party towards universal suffrage and legislation for the benefit of the working class. There were as yet no Socialists to speak of, and the prominent trade union leaders who supported the First International did so on account of its advocacy of international labour co-operation and not because they had any sympathy for the tenets of Marxism.

There was little basic difference of political philosophy, therefore, between the working-class Radicals and the keener reformers in Parliament, except that very few of the latter would have gone so far as to approve of manhood suffrage. But their arguments in favour of the principle of reform were the same. George Howell, the secretary of the Reform League and a well-known trade union leader, turned one of Bright's analogics against the more timid Liberal reformers. "Shame on Englishmen," he wrote, "who can see Germany enfranchized as well as the late slave states of America and still go on plastering and patching."[1] Like Bright and his Parliamentary allies, the working-class politicians had nothing but enthusiasm for American institutions, and were naturally quick to emphasize their advantages for members of their own class. Thus C. J. Bunting, President of the Norwich Political Union, in a pamphlet called *A Working Man's Reply* drew attention to the observations of travellers in America that there was no unemployment or destitution there;[2] and the Scottish section of the Reform League, in an address to "The People of Scotland," sought to prove the excellence of democratic government by quoting the statistics of economic growth in America since 1840—no doubt a telling argument with their money-wise compatriots.[3]

The most important organ of working-class opinion was *Reynolds's Newspaper*, a weekly published in London by a former Chartist. Its leading columns of this period reveal a partisan enthusiasm for American institutions that can only be paralleled

[1] To W. F. Johnston, 21 Dec. 1866, Reform League Letter-books, Howell Collection, Bishopsgate Institute, London.
[2] C. J. Bunting, *A Working Man's Reply* (Norwich, 1866), p. 10.
[3] Scottish National Reform League, *Address* (Glasgow, 1867).

in modern times by the enthusiasm of the Communist *Daily Worker* for the Soviet way of life. But *Reynolds's* was much more important and representative than the *Worker* is. In 1861 its circulation was 350,000, at a time when the daily circulation of *The Times* was only 70,000,[1] and there was no labour newspaper in any position to challenge it. *Reynolds's* had no doubt that in America all was for the best:

> We find that the men most distinguished for their eloquence, learning, statesmanship, naval and military ability, are entrusted with the management of the civil, political, naval and military affairs of the republic. In England, however, the reverse of all this is the case.[2]

When *The Times* criticized American congressmen as mere delegates, who voted as their constituents ordered by telegraph,[3] there was an outburst of wrath from *Reynolds's*:

> What is the member for Calne [Lowe] but the delegate of the Marquis of Lansdowne? What the member for Woodstock [Henry Barnett, a Conservative], but the delegate of the Duke of Marlborough? . . . They are almost all delegates, like the members of the United States Congress; with this difference—that the latter are the agents of free and independent communities, whereas the former are the delegates, lackeys, and dirty tools of insolent, small-brained, feeble-minded and freedom-hating aristocrats.[4]

Although it was true enough that plenty of corruption and "influence" still existed in the British electoral system, much of the polemic of *Reynolds's* outran the facts, and can have had little weight with those who were swayed by the arguments of the Adullamites. But its leader-writers could certainly preach most effectively to those already converted. One typically vigorous counter-attack was directed against the view that the American system bred mediocrity in statesmen. The writer quoted the case of Lord Northbrook, sometime Chancellor of the Exchequer and First Lord of the Admiralty, but nevertheless, according to *The Times* obituary, a man of only moderate gifts, whose wealth had brought him to a position of importance. "This," said the author

---

[1] E. L. Woodward, *The Age of Reform* (Oxford, 1938), p. 601.
[2] *Reynolds's Newspaper*, 9 Sept. 1866.   [3] *The Times*, 7 Sept. 1866.
[4] *Reynolds's Newspaper*, 16 Sept. 1866.

of the *Reynolds's* article, "is the secret of all official and governmental eminence in England."[1]

There were no reservations to the constant stream of eulogy which *Reynolds's* poured upon American institutions. The paper did not hesitate to advocate republicanism with a frankness of utterance that would be highly unpopular today:

> The Americans do not expend nearly a million per annum in the support of royalty, they do not grant pensions to foreign powers, and they are not asked to give enormous allowances to an interminable fry of native princes and princesses.[2]

Language of this sort was not infrequent in a period when the Crown had ceased to play an important part in domestic politics but had not yet fully developed its ceremonial role. Extreme Radicals of the time, attaching great importance as they did to purely political reforms, could see no advantages in the retention of the monarchy; and the Queen, living in widowed seclusion and attending very few public functions, did little to encourage the idea that she was a valuable element in the constitution.

If we turn to the *Beehive*, the smaller weekly controlled by George Potter of the London Working Men's Association, we find an attitude to America very similar to that of *Reynolds's*. Potter was especially interested in the status of labour in the United States. Referring to the eight-hours movement there, he wrote in 1866:

> Our American brethren have a more correct knowledge of the duties belonging to them as men; a higher estimate of the dignity and rights of labour; arising possibly from the fact that they are treated as free men and citizens in their native land, and not as helots, whom it would be unsafe to trust with the franchise.

And he went on to praise the educational facilities afforded to workmen in America, and the extensive labour press that existed there.[3]

In January 1867 both *Reynolds's* and the *Beehive* carried reports of two lectures delivered to the Working Men's Institute of Edinburgh, the first by J. S. Blackie, the Professor of Greek at the University, and the second, which was in the nature of a reply to

---

[1] *Reynolds's Newspaper*, 16 Sept. 1866.   [2] *Ibid.*, 16 Dec. 1866.
[3] *Beehive*, 13 Jan. 1866.

the first, by Ernest Jones, the former Chartist leader who was a Vice-President of the Reform League.[1] The subject of both lectures was "Democracy," but America was naturally a principal topic in the discussion. The professor spoke of the American enthusiasm for material prosperity; Jones retorted by pointing to the idealism of the struggle against slavery, and to the impressive expenditure on free libraries, free schools, and university education. The professor referred to rowdyism and corruption in New York and to the bribery of the legislature at Albany; Jones declared that New York was exceptional, consisting as it did of "the Romish-Irish, the refuse of your monarchies and aristocracies, the men whom you have degraded by your class rule." Taken as a whole, said Jones, America was the best-educated nation in the world, possessed of a "great constellation of order-loving, moral, and prosperous municipalities."[2] For this speech the *Beehive* had nothing but praise; and *Reynolds's* had only this fault to find: "He seemed to apologize a little too much for New York. . . . In New York, men do not die of cold and hunger in the streets—events of almost daily occurrence in London."[3]

It will be apparent that the working-class Radicals, like Bright, were happy to regard America as the prototype of the democratic utopia. The criticisms of such writers as De Tocqueville, who emphasized the mediocrity of American political leadership, and Dickens, who stressed the vulgarity of American manners, had some weight with the authors of *Essays on Reform*, who were members of the educated *élite*, but the working men of Britain, excluded as they were both from advanced education and from the suffrage, could not be expected to feel the force of such arguments. They knew that large numbers of their relatives and friends had emigrated to America, that few of these ever returned home, and that even those who returned usually had much to say in praise of the opportunity and freedom of working-class life across the Atlantic. Throughout the 1860's the average annual total of emigrants from the United Kingdom was 168,000, and it

---

[1] Reports of the lectures were published separately at Edinburgh in 1867: J. S. Blackie, *On Democracy*, and Ernest Jones, *Democracy Vindicated*.

[2] Jones, *op. cit.*, p. 12.

[3] *Beehive*, 12 Jan. 1867; *Reynolds's Newspaper*, 13 Jan. 1867.

is noteworthy that nearly three-quarters of them went to the United States.[1]

It would be a laborious task to trace in detail the influence of the reports sent home by the emigrants, or the impact of those who returned. Thomas Wright, a journeyman engineer, was one of the very few authors of the time to write about working-class life from personal experience: he tells us that he had an opportunity to read many letters received by friends and kinsmen of emigrants. "They say that the portion and chances of the working men are substantially better than here, and working men more thought of."[2] This probably sums up the experience of most who went and of many who returned, although criticism among the latter was naturally more common. John Wilson, a miner who spent some years in Pennsylvania during the Civil War, but who returned and eventually became a Liberal-Labour M.P., wrote of the freedom and social equality that he encountered in the mining villages. "The highest citizen was not a long way up," he wrote. "There was no need for a social telescope to see him."[3] James Burn, the self-styled "Beggar Boy," whose stay in America must roughly have concided with Wilson's, was less generally enthusiastic than Wilson but agreed with him as to the existence of social equality.[4] The best evidence of this social equality, for those who compared British and American institutions, was the American common school system, and the pages of the Radical press often contained eulogies of the "training for life," received by young Americans "at an age when children in England were, through parental poverty, in the workshop, competing with and injuring adult labour, growing up ignorant and stunted, intellectually and physically."[5]

Thus the democratic faith of the British artisan, tried by the touchstone of his own personal experiences and those of his kinsfolk across the Atlantic, made him in these years the staunchest

[1] Brinley Thomas, *Migration and Economic Growth* (Cambridge, 1954), p. 57.
[2] Thomas Wright, *Our New Masters* (London, 1873), p. 31.
[3] John Wilson, *Memories of a Labour Leader* (London, 1910), p. 167.
[4] "Beggar Boy" (James Burn), *Three Years among the Working Classes of the United States During the War* (London, 1865), p. xii. He also commented on the paucity of pawnbrokers in America, *ibid.*, p. x.
[5] *National Reformer*, 14 Oct. 1866.

of all the European supporters of the institutions of the United States. It was symbolical that at the mass reform demonstrations in London "Yankee Doodle" and "John Brown" were sung,[1] and that the processions made courtesy calls upon the American minister, Charles Francis Adams—somewhat to his embarrassment, for he realized that this might open him to the charge of intervening in British domestic politics.[2] Adams was sensible of the compliment paid to America for her example; but he was also shrewd enough to realize that it carried a heavy responsibility with it, for it was an indication of high hopes for the future of the democratic experiment in his country. Writing at a time of acute conflict between President and Congress, it is understandable that he allowed a note of warning to creep into his report to Secretary Seward at Washington:

There is still something to be done to prove to the world that the recuperative power of the people is not wasted away in internal strife and the protracted indulgence of hostile passions. The example is necessary to Great Britain, as it is to all the continental nations which are peacefully struggling towards the end of intelligent self-government, to encourage them to persevere. I trust that it may not be long before it can be brought to shine out in its fullest splendor.[3]

*   *   *

The idealism expressed so eloquently by Lincoln found ready response among British Radicals, and in the two years after his death, little concern for current American political difficulties or future economic problems marred their enthusiasm for the constitutional panacea of democracy on the transatlantic pattern. If more cautious Liberals like Gladstone eschewed the American parallel, its importance was magnified by the attention paid to it as a bogey by the opponents of reform. And since the Civil War had ended in the triumph of the Union, the American example, being a rallying-point for the forces of British Radicalism, played its part in setting Britain further and more decisively upon the path that led to full democracy.

[1] *Reynolds's Newspaper*, 17 Feb. 1867; Thomas Frost, *Forty Years' Recollections* (London, 1880), p. 309.
[2] Adams to Seward, 13 Feb. 1867, *Papers Relating to Foreign Affairs*, Second Session, 40th Congress, Part 1 (Washington, D.C., 1868), p. 63.
[3] Adams to Seward, 9 Aug. 1867, *op. cit.*, p. 123.

CHAPTER III

THE LIBERAL PARTY "AMERICANIZED"

THE extension of the franchise by the legislation of 1867 impressed upon the governing classes in Britain the need for certain consequential measures. Civil service reform, to establish the principle of competitive entry, was carried into force by Order in Council with almost universal agreement, in order to forestall any development of a spoils system of the American type. Popular education on a universal basis was a necessary corollary of a popular electorate, and the Liberal Government's Education Act of 1870 laid the groundwork for a national system. In addition, without any further executive or legislative action, the growth of the electorate brought with it a vast extension of party organization in which again certain parallels with American practice could be observed. The civil service reforms went through with little discussion: but the question of popular education challenged many susceptibilities, and here much controversy arose. In the course of public activity on this question we can see the beginnings of the rapid growth of extra-parliamentary party organization, which aroused fresh issues in its turn, and caused the state of America to be debated once more with almost as much vigour as in 1866–7.

It was the religious question that lay at the root of the differences over education. As the Church of England had a considerable advantage in the number of its existing schools, the nonconformists were anxious to defeat any plans based on a subsidy of voluntary schools. One of them, Jesse Collings of Birmingham, who had first entered politics as a supporter of the North in the Civil War, wrote a pamphlet urging the establishment of something like the American school system in England.[1] He proposed the formation of a society to agitate for this end. The pamphlet was based on the description of the American common school

---

[1] J. Collings, *An Outline of the American Schools System: with Remarks on the Establishment of Common Schools in England* (Birmingham, 1868); J. Collings and J. L. Green, *Life of Jesse Collings* (London, 1920), p. 80.

system given in the report of the Rev. James Fraser, who had been commissioned by the government to visit America in 1865 for that purpose.[1]

The American common school, and in particular the type in operation in Massachusetts, had long been the British Radicals' ideal of educational reform.[2] But Collings was speaking for a group of Birmingham dissenters, all members of the Liberal Party, who in the succeeding years mobilized nonconformist opinion as a political pressure group in a way that was without precedent in British politics. The most important member of the group was Joseph Chamberlain, a Unitarian, who also valued the American experience of a compulsory non-denominational system, and was in touch with Americans such as William Emerson of Concord, the brother of Ralph Waldo Emerson.[3] Chamberlain, who had gained political experience in organizing the Birmingham Liberals so effectively as to overcome the minority provisions of the Reform Act, now took the lead in forming the "National Education League" as a pressure group of the nonconformist interest. The provisional committee was composed of George Dixon, one of the three Liberal M.P.s for Birmingham, as Chairman, Chamberlain as Vice-Chairman, and Collings as Honorary Secretary. The committee rapidly collected funds, and began to press the Liberal government to adopt a policy based upon the proposals of Colling's pamphlet.

Almost immediately, however, there came into existence a rival body formed to support the Anglican interest, and known as the National Education Union;[4] and it soon became clear that the dissenting view would not easily prevail. W. E. Forster, who was the Minister responsible for educational policy, though brought

[1] Fraser's "Report on the Common School System" is to be found in *Parliamentary Papers* (1867), xxvi, 293–759. As a supporter of voluntary and denominational schools, his conclusion is interesting: he regarded America as "if not the most *highly* educated, yet certainly the most *generally* educated and intelligent people on the earth." (*Ibid.*, 499.) Fraser became Bishop of Manchester in 1870.

[2] G. D. Lillibridge, *Beacon of Freedom*, pp. 97 ff.

[3] J. L. Garvin, *Life of Joseph Chamberlain* (London, 1932), i, 91.

[4] See National Education Union, *Authorized Report of Educational Congress* (London, 1869), which contains a fierce denunciation of American education and politics by Lord Robert Montagu, M.P., a Conservative ex-minister.

up as a Quaker, had been ejected from that community for marrying an Anglican—in fact, Matthew Arnold's sister. Matthew Arnold himself, who was deeply interested in the problems of education, was unsympathetic to Chamberlain's policy, and wrote to a relative of his:

The American schools do not interest me much, because, as in this country the *summum bonum* is to be a lord or a millionaire, in America the *summum bonum* is to be a millionaire, and culture cannot really make much way when that is the *summum bonum*. . . . Fraser has never seen the continental schools.[1]

Forster's proposals were certainly unsatisfactory to the leaders of the National Education League. Although he accepted the aim of establishing universal elementary education, he at first proposed to base his scheme upon the voluntary schools, allowing scholars to obtain exemption from religious teaching if their parents so desired. The League naturally objected strongly, and Forster was obliged to set up popularly elected school boards to control the schools established by the government. In its final form, however, the measure increased the existing support given to denominational schools, and Chamberlain and his friends felt that Forster had foiled them of the system which they desired, and indeed regarded as essential for the survival of their congregations. It counted for little with the dissenters that Forster, in his five years in office, had secured an increase of the number of schools by 60 per cent.[2] The opposition continued after the Act was passed, and John Bright, while actually a member of the government, repudiated Forster's work in a speech at Birmingham.[3] These conflicts weakened the Liberal Party and contributed to its defeat in the 1874 General Election.

Chamberlain's work in the National Education League marked him out as a politician of considerable ability, and his reforms of municipal government in Birmingham during his three years as mayor in 1873–6 enabled him to lay claim to the leadership of the Radical wing of the party. Forster's position was seriously weak-

[1] To Russell Martineau, 21 June 1867, quoted Garvin, *op. cit.*, i, 91.
[2] W. H. G. Armytage, "W. E. Forster and the Liberal Reformers," in A. V. Judges (ed.), *Pioneers of English Education* (London, 1952), p. 214.
[3] T. Wemyss Reid, *Life of W. E. Forster* (London, 1888), i, 556.

ened by the hostility of the nonconformists, who had by their opposition prevented him from succeeding as leader of the party when Gladstone retired early in 1875. Rather than Forster, the nonconformist Radicals accepted the Whig Lord Hartington as the party leader. This left the way open for Chamberlain to rise rapidly to national prominence as soon as he was elected to Parliament, which took place at a by-election in 1876 when George Dixon retired. His aim was now to supersede the Education League with a national organization of Liberal Associations, which was to be based on Birmingham. Early in 1877 he was making plans for the establishment of the new body, which was to be known as the National Liberal Federation.[1]

It was one thing for Chamberlain to advocate an educational system corresponding to that in America, which to say the least compared favourably with that of England; it was another thing for him to seek to extend extra-Parliamentary political machinery, for this savoured of American politics, which more than ever were regarded in Britain as debased and corrupt. The prejudices of the previous decade had been reinforced, not only by the consciousness of superiority afforded by the introduction of competitive examinations for Civil Service entry by the Order in Council of 1870, but also by the repeated evidence from across the Atlantic of the Republican Party's loss of idealism since the Civil War. It was the political atmosphere of these years which provided the background for Mark Twain's *Gilded Age* and Henry Adams's *Democracy*. In 1875 the Democrats, having won the House in the mid-term elections, instituted investigations of Republican administration which revealed some startling scandals. State and city government were also in a bad way: the Tweed Ring and the Gas Ring were notorious in New York and Philadelphia respectively. One of the principal opponents of the former was the editor of the *New York Times*, Louis J. Jennings, an Englishman

---

[1] For the origins of the Federation see M. Ostrogorski, *Democracy and the Organization of Political Parties* (London, 1902); and F. H. Herrick, "The Origin of the National Liberal Federation," *Journal of Modern History*, xvii (1945), 116–29. For its absorption of the National Education League in 1877, see Francis Adams, *The History of the Elementary School System* (London, 1882), p. 329. Adams, who was the secretary of the League, had published a volume entitled *The Free School System of the United States* (London, 1875).

who had formerly been the American correspondent of the London *Times*. Indigenous critics of corruption were not lacking, however, and their activity led to the selection of Hayes and Tilden as candidates for the Presidential election of 1876, and to a degree of administrative reform under Hayes, who emerged the victor. Hayes had to contend with a senatorial cabal led by Conkling, who bitterly but on the whole unsuccessfully opposed the reform of the New York customs in 1877-8. It was thus just at the moment when for the first time something was being done to deal with the problem of corruption in American politics that Englishmen became most fully aware of it; and, as in the previous decade, some of them were prepared to attribute it to the existence of democratic institutions in general and to extra-Parliamentary political machinery in particular.

★   ★   ★

The inaugural conference of the National Liberal Federation was held at a great meeting at Birmingham on 31st May, 1877. The climax of the demonstration was a speech on the Eastern Question by Gladstone, whom Chamberlain had induced to attend. This was the starting-point of a growing apprehension among the members of the old governing class about the significance of the new organization. *The Times*, in a leader on 12th June, remarked with evident concern:

There is to be a sort of Liberal Parliament organized, which, in American language, seems intended to act as a Liberal "Caucus."

Although the Federation corresponded more directly to an American "convention" than to a "caucus," the latter word was no doubt revived for the sake of its vague suggestions of wire-pulling by a minority of unscrupulous politicians.

The *Saturday Review* was equally convinced that the Federation would end in "American vulgarity and corruption."[1] Chamberlain retorted that the epithet "caucus" had been devised by "those who distrust the people";[2] but in fact it was not only the opponents of democracy who reacted in this way. Goldwin Smith, the fierce "American" Radical of only a decade earlier, who had lived in

[1] *Saturday Review*, 16 June 1877.
[2] J. Chamberlain, "A New Political Organization," *Fortnightly Review*, n.s., xxii (July 1877), p. 134.

America for several years and was now in Canada, had become sufficiently disillusioned about certain aspects of American political life to write in *Macmillan's Magazine*:

> We must say that the use of such machinery does seem to involve a terrible sacrifice of those very habits of mental independence which it is the pride of Liberalism to promote. The absolute necessity of defending progress and the interests of the community at large against the despotism of a class alone reconciles us in any measure to the system. In the United States the masters of the party machine have everywhere taken the representation out of the hands of the people; you are practically not at liberty to vote for anyone but their nominees; and the Republican horse, to vanquish the Democratic stag, becomes absolutely the slave of its rider.[1]

Goldwin Smith had evidently had second thoughts since the controversies of the previous decade, but the views of his old opponent Robert Lowe had not changed at all. "America," said Lowe in the same year, "seems to have been called into existence for our instruction," and he cited the maltreatment of the Indians, the adherence to the "exploded errors of Protection," and the corruption of the Civil Service in America as the three principal arguments to prove that the United States was not as well governed as Britain.[2]

As the organization of the local Liberal associations on the Birmingham model proceeded in 1877, the alarm of the aristocratic elements in both the Liberal and Conservative parties began to grow. Early in November Chamberlain addressed a Liberal meeting in Rochdale in order to explain the "Birmingham plan," and John Bright took the chair. Commenting on Bright's observations, *The Times* remarked:

> He describes an organization as compact, as tyrannical, as unprincipled, and as injurious to this country as the Ottoman Power in the midst of so many subject, though better, races.[3]

[1] Goldwin Smith, "The Decline of Party Government," *Macmillan's Magazine*, xxxvi (Aug. 1877), p. 302.

[2] R. Lowe, "A New Reform Bill," *Fortnightly Review*, n.s., xxii (Oct. 1877), p. 446.

[3] *The Times*, 9 Nov. 1877. The approval of this leader may have been one of the last editorial acts of J. T. Delane, who retired on the previous day after being editor of *The Times* since 1841.—A. I. Dasent, *John Thaddeus Delane* (London, 1908), ii, 336.

The Whigs of the Liberal Party were especially embarrassed by Chamberlain's activity, which, they realized, was designed to strengthen the new Radical wing at the expense of themselves. Lord Hartington wrote to his colleague Lord Granville on 23rd November:

I do not feel at all certain that we ought to give in our adhesion to this federation scheme. . . . It is almost certain to put the management into the hand of the most advanced men, because they are the most active. . . . There is a good deal of the American caucus system about it, which I think is not liked here.[1]

Moderate Liberals and independent Radicals like Leonard Courtney could agree with the Whigs on this. Courtney, who as a *Times* leader-writer had fought for the representation of minorities in 1866–7, had discovered that the minority clause of the act could be rendered ineffective by elaborate local organization such as that of Chamberlain's Birmingham Liberal Association. In March 1878, as a Liberal M.P. himself, he moved in the Commons for the acceptance of the general principle of minority representation. Speaking of the National Liberal Federation, he said that he

could not conceive how any person who had any knowledge of the caucus system in the United States could look at the growth of that Confederation with any feelings other than those of apprehension. Its object was to repress local feeling, local energy, and independence.[2]

In April a writer in the Whig *Edinburgh Review* could still take comfort in the advantages of the English constitution over the American, saying that "caucuses in the American form are out of place among our comparatively small constituencies";[3] but the trend in favour of the Birmingham system was unmistakable, and the alarm at its growth steadily increased. In the *Nineteenth Century* of May W. Fraser Rae, a former American correspondent of the *Daily News*, remarked on the close comparison between the Birmingham method of selecting candidates and those that were prevalent in America: the only difference being in the names given

---

[1] B. Holland, *Life of Spencer Compton, Eighth Duke of Devonshire* (London, 1911), i, 245.

[2] *Parl. Deb.*, 3rd ser., ccxxxviii, 1010 f. (8 Mar. 1878). See also G. P. Gooch, *Life of Lord Courtney* (London, 1920), p. 142.

[3] *Edinburgh Review*, cxlvii (Apr. 1878), 332.

to the institutions concerned. The "primary meeting" and "nominating convention" of America, he said, were called the "ward meeting" and the "Six Hundred" in Birmingham. Rae sounded a warning against the further extension of the system in Britain, and applauded the protest of E. A. Leatham, Liberal M.P. for Huddersfield, who had told his constituents that he would sooner see his party "effaced altogether than that it should exist under the conditions of the parties of the United States."[1]

The "odious comparison" with American politics was now so frequent that it was only a matter of time before the term "caucus" came to be regarded as a synonym for the National Liberal Federation and its constituent bodies.[2] Although, as we have seen, the word could not be applied to the Federation in its strict American sense, the opportunity to use an opprobrious epithet was not let slip simply because it was inexact: and the parallel in any case was felt to be close.

It was the Conservative Prime Minister, Benjamin Disraeli, now Lord Beaconsfield, who, more than anyone else, was responsible for branding the Federation once and for all as the "caucus." The debate on the Eastern Question, and Gladstone's merciless criticism of the government's foreign policy, had aroused bitter hostility between the two great statesmen, which culminated in an exchange of letters in July, 1878, after an accusation by Beaconsfield that Gladstone had described him as "devilish." In the course of a reply to a request from Gladstone asking for details of this charge, Beaconsfield referred to "the Birmingham caucus";[3] and as soon as the correspondence was in print the denunciations of the Federation rose to a climax. *The Times* declared:

There is no magic in the English nature to keep us free from the evils to which politics in the United States have succumbed. The process may be slower here, and it may be specially arrested in those parts of the country where the traditions of old associations are most powerful, but it is not in such places that the Birmingham system has

[1] *Nineteenth Century*, iii (May 1878), 922 f., 931. Rae had visited America for the Centennial of the Declaration of Independence in 1876, and had written a book on his return, *Columbia and Canada* (London, 1877).

[2] For a useful, if incomplete, discussion of the English usage of the word "caucus," see *Notes and Queries*, 8th ser., vi (1894), 309 f.

[3] *The Times*, 31 July 1878; reprinted in W. F. Monypenny and G. E. Buckle, *Life of Benjamin Disraeli, Earl of Beaconsfield*, vi (1920), 358.

D

spread or is likely to spread. It is in boroughs like Smethwick, and Greenwich, and Marylebone that the principle will have free action, and it is there that it is first introduced.[1]

The Times was right in expecting the principal development of the new system to take place in the larger boroughs. The extensive electorates created by household suffrage provided the political organizers with a great opportunity. The country constituencies, on the other hand, were less favourable, for the old type of "influence" was still of importance, and even after the Ballot Act of 1872 landlords could find ways of controlling the votes of their tenants.

But the protagonists of the National Liberal Federation naturally could not let The Times's criticisms of their work go unchallenged. Chamberlain himself at once wrote to the editor:

> I observe that you, in common with the Prime Minister, have adopted the "caucus" to designate our organization. The sting does not lie in the original meaning of this word, but in its modern acceptance as involving the idea of corruption unfortunately associated with American politics.[2]

Chamberlain went on to suggest that this corruption was caused not by the "representative system of organization" but by the extent of the spoils system, which did not apply to England. Thus the new Radical leader made a concession which many of his predecessors had been unwilling to make—that in one respect, at least, the British polity was better than the American.

It was in vain, however, that Chamberlain attacked the use of the word "caucus." There was no escaping it; and only a few days later The Times, whose staff was evidently enjoying the controversy,[3] published the correspondence between Alfred Illingworth, the leader of the new Bradford Liberal Association, and W. E. Forster, who was M.P. for Bradford. It was clear that Illingworth was attempting to compel Forster to adopt the policy of the

---

[1] The Times, 31 July 1878.   [2] Ibid., 1 Aug. 1878.
[3] Henry James, writing on "London in the Dead Season" in the New York Nation of 26 Sept. 1878, said: "I am ignorant whether The Times receives during the months of August and September a greater number of confidential epistles from the injured or the gratified, the disappointed, the swindled, the inquisitive, or the communicative Briton, but it certainly prints a great many more."

Association, which was dominated by the nonconformists.[1] The day after the correspondence was published, *The Times* printed a letter from an anonymous American, urging the people of Britain to avoid adopting American political machinery along with the more useful novelties such as "sewing machines, and agricultural implements, and tramways," which were coming from across the Atlantic.[2]

At this point Francis Schnadhorst, the secretary of the National Liberal Federation, entered the controversy in self-defence. Schnadhorst had worked for Chamberlain's political creations in turn: he had been secretary both of the Central Nonconformist Committee and of the Birmingham Liberal Association. In letters to *The Times* he argued that the Bradford Liberal Association was a special case, and that there was nothing improper about the Federation as a whole.[3] Forster himself refused to believe that his own case was a unique one: early in September he wrote privately to Gladstone, suggesting that it was Birmingham that was the exception, and that the Bradford association was nearer the "probable pattern of caucus activity." He believed that any permanent committees in the constituencies would normally be unrepresentative, and that they would "degenerate into wire-pullers, as in the States, or, as in Bradford, represent the agitation for disestablishment, or some such special question."[4]

Forster's comparison with the situation in America probably carried weight with Gladstone, who knew that Forster had visited the United States in 1874, and may have known that he had actually attended a caucus meeting of Tammany.[5] But it is clear from Gladstone's own references to American politics at this time that he regarded corruption as a mild and superficial blemish on an otherwise healthy body politic;[6] and other Liberal M.P.s who

[1] *The Times*, 12 Aug. 1878. *Punch* of 24 Aug. contained the conundrum: "Why is Mr. Forster like the Czar?" with the answer, "Because he declines to be stopped by the Caucusses."

[2] *The Times*, 13 Aug. 1878.   [3] *Ibid.*, 20 and 23 Aug. 1878.

[4] To Gladstone, 2 Sept. 1878: reprinted in Reid, *Life of W. E. Forster*, p. 434.

[5] *Ibid.*, p. 356 f.

[6] See especially his article "Kin Beyond Sea," *North American Review*, cxxvii (Sept.–Oct. 1878), pp. 179–211. Gladstone was most impressed by the speed with which "the most unmitigated democracy known to the annals of the world" had reduced its public debt (*ibid.*, p. 189).

had visited America failed to see any grave threat to British institutions in the "caucus" system. Charles Dilke, for instance, who was to be a close associate of Chamberlain's, turned a deaf ear to a request from the Duchess of Manchester that he should "back up Mr. Forster,"[1] for, as he later declared, he was "an absolute believer in the wisdom of the Caucus," and he claimed to have founded an association of the "caucus" type in Chelsea, his own constituency, before the Birmingham association was founded.[2]

In September, however, the arguments of the critics of the "caucus" received support from an article in the New York *Nation*, which was then edited by the British-born and Anglophile E. L. Godkin. The article described the new associations and forecast their future in American terms: the Birmingham "Six Hundred" was like the "Tammany General Committee," and as the interest of its members flagged, the real power, it was suggested, would pass to the local "Boss." It was true, of course, that there was no spoils system in England: but such a satisfactory state of affairs could not last. This gloomy prognosis arrived in London too late for the immediate controversy in *The Times*, but in good time for the more leisurely debate which continued in the periodicals.[3]

The *Nineteenth Century* was not slow in re-entering the fray. In October there appeared an article by E. D. J. Wilson, who was actually a member of *The Times's* staff. Wilson threw some much-needed light on the real meaning of the word "caucus." He pointed out that in America it meant "a secret meeting of a Parliamentary Party, intended to decide upon a course of political action," whereas the Birmingham "Grand Committee," which was now being called a "caucus," would be known in the United States as a "political convention." Still, Wilson felt that the general analogy held good. If adopted, the new organization would "develop all the evils which have degraded and defeated popular

[1] Dilke Papers, B.M. Add. Mss. 43885 f. 123.
[2] *Ibid.*, 43925 f. 259; S. Gwynn and G. M. Tuckwell, *Life of Sir Charles Dilke* (London, 1917), i, 268. Dilke had visited America in 1866 and had formed a not unfavourable view of American politics. See his *Greater Britain* (London, 1868), i, 292.
[3] *Nation*, xxvii, 141 f. (5 Sept. 1878).

government in the United States." Nor could he accept the view that these evils in America depended upon the existence of the spoils system:

The Democrats of Massachusetts, for example, have no share either in the Federal or the State patronage, yet their conventions are as strictly ruled by the "machine-men," and are as hostile to the political existence of the independent voter, as they are in New York itself.

Such being the case, the "machine" would triumph in Britain as it had in America: like the "Car of Juggernaut" it would crush down all individuality and independence, and politicians like Senator Conkling of New York and Senator Cameron of Pennsylvania would rule the land.[1]

Wilson's gloom about American politics was soon challenged. Edward R. Russell, writing in the Liverpool *Daily Post* which he edited, suggested that President Hayes's moves for reform were evidence that the "caucus" could not for long run counter to public opinion. He also maintained that the absence of a spoils system in Britain was a much more important difference between the two countries than Wilson would admit.[2] In the meantime, Chamberlain himself had been stimulated to re-define his position. He accepted the invitation of John Morley, the Liberal editor of the *Fortnightly Review*, to write an article for the November issue. He decided to abandon the attitude of apology for American institutions that he had adopted in his letter to *The Times*, and to challenge the basic assumptions of the critics of the "caucus." He wrote to Morley on 1st October.

As to the line I shall take, I am afraid you will not think it very persuasive, but I feel that the time for anything like apology is passed. ... The case of our opponents rests on three assumptions—1st, that the system of local and national Government in America is corrupt and degraded; 2nd, that this is due to the Caucus; 3rd, that the Birmingham system is the same as the American and will lead to the same alleged results. All these assumptions I dispute.[3]

The article, in its published form, follows out this plan. Some politicians in America, admitted Chamberlain, were of poor

---

[1] *Nineteenth Century*, iv (Oct. 1878), 698, 701, 708.
[2] Liverpool *Daily Post*, 10 Oct. 1878; Russell to Gladstone, 10 Oct. 1878, Gladstone Papers, B.M. Add. Mss. 44458 ff. 41–4.
[3] Garvin, *Life of J. Chamberlain*, i, 263.

quality: the same, however, was true of politicians of other countries. It was true that many educated men deliberately abstained from public life there: but this was due to concentration on business and to "the fact that the greater issues of politics have long ago been settled." Here emerged the old Radical admiration for the American social system:

A nation which has no Land question, no Church question, no Education question and no Foreign Policy, must purchase its advantages at the price of less sustained and vital interest in its legislative work.[1]

Chamberlain then proceeded to deal with the second assumption of his opponents, and urged that the "caucus" was not responsible for whatever was at fault in America. "In truth . . . the caucus protects individuality and secures independence against tyranny." The value of the new system was that it ensured that the majority should rule, instead of the minority.

It is because minorities, and often very small minorities, have had such power in determining the course of English politics, that such deep hostility is shown by a minority to a system which is avowedly designed to relieve majorities from the disabilities under which they have so long laboured.[2]

Finally, Chamberlain came to the third assumption. He repeated the point which he had originally made in writing to *The Times*, and which Edward Russell had also emphasized: that there was no spoils system in England, and that this was the real cause of corruption in America. He also referred to the article in the New York *Nation*, and pointed out that there was no question in Birmingham of the public interest beginning to flag, thereby allowing the introduction of a "Boss."

These arguments evidently satisfied Gladstone, who continued to give his support to the "Birmingham plan." But the "caucus" did not work equally well in all the constituencies where it was attempted. A by-election which took place at Peterborough just at the moment when Chamberlain's article appeared considerably discredited the system, for the chosen candidate of the "caucus"—

[1] J. Chamberlain, "The Caucus," *Fortnightly Review*, n.s., xxiv, 723 f.
[2] *Ibid.*, 726 f.

a representative of the nonconformist interest—was soundly defeated by a Whig-Liberal and, with a Conservative also standing, secured less than a quarter of the poll in what was a strongly Liberal constituency. Gladstone, speaking at Greenwich at the end of November, drew a distinction between a broadly-based association like that of Birmingham, which satisfactorily performed the important function of choosing Liberal candidates, and such a body as the Peterborough association, composed "after some hugger-mugger fashion" which was not truly representative. Gladstone deplored the fact that the Liberal vote had been split in so many constituencies in the 1874 election, and argued:

It is rather hard on Mr. Wright [chairman of the Birmingham Liberal Association] and his friends at Birmingham that ugly words should be brought across the Atlantic and thrown at their heads because they have endeavoured to apply a remedy to a state of things so discreditable to them as men of sense.[1]

But the Whigs remained unconvinced. Hartington refused further pressure from Chamberlain to appear at a meeting of the Federation at Leeds;[2] and the *Edinburgh Review* (whose editor was the translator of De Tocqueville, Henry Reeve) refused to believe that any "caucus" could be representative. After all, it argued, the system had hardly been tried at Birmingham, for of the three Birmingham M.P.s, neither Bright nor Muntz, nor even Chamberlain himself, could really be regarded as nominees of the "caucus."[3] *The Times*, returning to the attack, agreed with this view, and quoted its American correspondent on the shameful state of the Philadelphia "caucus," which was "a mere apparatus for registering foregone conclusions."[4] One Liberal politician— none other than G. C. Brodrick, one of the contributors to the 1867 *Essays on Reform*—wrote up to say that he could not submit himself to the indignity of public examination by a "caucus" before nomination as parliamentary candidate. Brodrick wrote

1 *The Times*, 2 Dec. 1878. Gladstone also stated the case for self-discipline of the Liberal Party in an article entitled "Electoral Facts," *Nineteenth Century*, iv (Nov. 1878), 955–68.
2 Holland, *Life of D. of Devonshire*, i, 245–8.
3 *Edinburgh Review*, cxlix (Jan. 1879), 263.
4 *The Times*, 25 Jan. and 27 Feb. 1879.

that the "caucus" depended for its justification "upon a degree of political virtue in its managers which American experience forbids us to expect."[1]

Nevertheless, the Federation continued to grow, and when its Council meeting took place at Leeds in January 1879, over a hundred associations had joined. Chamberlain could play the part of Radical spokesman and critic of the Whigs, especially as Hartington had refused his invitation to attend. Although Chamberlain had resigned himself to the name "caucus," which, coming from Beaconsfield, he was "inclined to take as a compliment," he was acidly critical of the *Edinburgh Review*, which had maintained that the Liberal party should have no committed programme for domestic affairs—an attitude, said Chamberlain, that would make the two parties like Tweedledum and Tweedledee.[2]

★   ★   ★

Although the main conflict was between the rising non-conformist interest, which formed the backbone of the Federation, and the Whigs of the old governing class, there was another group inside the Liberal party which was as apprehensive as the Whigs of the effects of "caucus" control, but, unlike the Whigs, was a growing and not a weakening force. This was the labour interest. Superficially, it is true, its political strength had changed surprisingly little since the passing of the 1867 Reform Act. Most of the leaders of the Reform League had transferred their energies to a new political association called the Labour Representation League, the object of which was to elect working men as Members of Parliament: but so far only two such men had been successful— Alexander Macdonald for Stafford and Thomas Burt for Morpeth, both of them miners. The trade union movement was suffering setbacks in the later eighteen-seventies, and proposals for candidatures sponsored by union funds met with a chilly response at a time when the unions were fighting for their lives against severe economic depression. The principal press organ of the labour interest was still *Reynolds's Newspaper*, and Potter's *Beehive* lived

[1] *The Times*, 13 Jan. 1879; G. C. Brodrick, *Political Studies* (London, 1879), p. 271.
[2] *The Times*, 23 Jan. 1879.

on under the name of the *Industrial Review*. By and large, their viewpoint was more closely wedded to that of the Liberal Party than it had been ten years earlier, when the party itself was only just attaining a degree of coherence after the death of Palmerston.

The attitude of British labour towards the United States had changed but little in the preceding decade. There was still no Socialism in England, as *Reynolds's Newspaper* pointed out in June 1878 when the subject was under discussion because of its rapid development in Germany.[1] In spite of the American industrial depression in the later eighteen-seventies and the consequent unemployment, which caused a temporary slump in migration, especially of the unskilled, the British working man continued to regard the United States as providing the most favourable opportunities for himself and his family.[2] Thus, for instance, the secretary of the Friendly Society of Ironfounders, who between 1874 and 1878 had been obliged to withhold the financial support customarily given to members emigrating to America, looked forward in 1878 to the time when America would again become "the land of Goshen for the dispossessed sons of toil in the old country."[3] The man who told Robert Louis Stevenson on board an emigrant ship in 1879 that "in America you get pies and puddings"[4] was translating into his own immediate terms the belief of a whole class, that across the Atlantic lay an "El Dorado of high wages," as Thomas Brassey, M.P., described it at the 1877 Trades Union Congress.[5]

The reports of political corruption in New York and elsewhere could hardly disturb such a general enthusiasm on the part of the working class. The outcry about the "caucus" as a dangerous Americanism therefore carried little weight with labour leaders. Lloyd Jones, the Radical and former Owenite, who was the first secretary of the Labour Representation League, dismissed the

---

[1] *Reynolds's Newspaper*, 23 June 1878.
[2] For emigration statistics see Brinley Thomas, *Migration and Economic Growth*, p. 282.
[3] Quoted in Charlotte Erickson, "Encouragement of Emigration by British Trade Unions," *Population Studies*, iii (1949), 271.
[4] R. L. Stevenson, *The Amateur Emigrant*, reprinted in *Works* (Tusitala ed., London, 1924), xviii, 64.
[5] T.U.C. *Report*, 1877, p. 24. Cf. leader in *Daily News*, 20 Aug. 1878.

suggestion as invalid in an article in the *Industrial Review*: those who argued that way, he said, "are simply dealing with a word, when in England we are interested in a thing which may or may not be worked in the same way as the caucus in America is worked." At the same time, the "caucus" worried labour men, for they were not at all sure that it would improve the chances of working-class candidatures for Parliament. "Borough caucuses," said Lloyd Jones,

would work admirably as traps in which to shut up the working men of the country, allowing them only such political action as their masters and managers may permit.[1]

"Gracchus," the columnist of *Reynolds's*, agreed. On the one hand, it would be a good thing to take the control of the constituencies out of the hands of the London political clubs; but the "caucus" system, even if it was satisfactory in America, could not work well in a class society like Britain.

It may be admirably adapted to the form of American society, but it is problematical how it will operate in a country where class distinctions are so broadly defined, and where every existing institution, clerical, political, and social, is so constituted as to increase the power of the powerful, and grind down the poor to the dust.

"Gracchus" concluded that the system might suit large towns, where the mass of voters would keep the control in popular hands, but would not do in less populous places, where influence and wealth would count more readily.[2] In fact, the working-class leaders made no condemnation of American politics, but limited themselves to scepticism about the democratic tendencies of their Liberal allies.

George Howell, who had been secretary of the Reform League during the great agitation of 1866-7, and was now on the executive of the Labour Representation League, expressed similar views in an article in the *New Quarterly Magazine*. He feared that each

[1] Lloyd Jones, "The Caucus Question and the Working Man," *Industrial Review*, 31 Aug. 1878.
[2] *Reynolds's Newspaper*, 1 Sept. 1878. "Gracchus," a pseudonym for a succession of writers, was probably at this time Edward Reynolds, the founder's brother and (from 1879 to 1894) his successor in the editorial chair.

association would cease to be truly representative and would get into the hands of a local clique, which would be worse than an American "caucus" could be.[1] This was the answer to Chamberlain's no doubt well-founded claim that in Birmingham at least the organization was "actually the whole Liberal constituency" and that "three-quarters of the great committee of the 600 are working-men."[2]

When the Peterborough by-election took place, the fears of the labour leaders seemed to find immediate justification; for George Potter, standing as a Liberal with the backing of the Labour Representation League, was rejected by the local "caucus" in favour of a zealot of the United Kingdom Alliance, a nonconformist temperance society. Howell wrote to the *Examiner* complaining of irregularities at the meeting of the "caucus" which made this decision,[3] and the final result of the election, which has already been mentioned, clearly indicated that it was not a representative body of the Liberal electors. Soon Howell was writing that "the caucus system is condemned by the major portion of the Liberal party. . . . We have found but comparatively few who have any faith at all in the scheme."[4]

It is clear that the working-class leaders had a very different objection to the "caucus" from that of Conservatives and Whigs. The latter felt that it was too "democratic," and, whether truly representative or not, would at any rate take power out of their own hands. The labour leaders, on the other hand, felt that it was not "democratic" enough, would become unrepresentative, and would fail to increase their own influence in the selection of Parliamentary candidates. Not that they had any alternative plan to offer as a means of securing due representation for all sections of the Liberal Party. It was sometimes suggested that if a "test ballot" of all Liberal electors were held in each constituency, the different interests of the party could prevail where they were strongest. This was something like the primary system, which the

---

[1] *New Quarterly Magazine*, x (Oct. 1878), 584.
[2] To Morley, 25 Nov. 1876, quoted Garvin, *Life of J. Chamberlain*, i, 258.
[3] *Examiner*, 26 Oct. 1878.
[4] *Industrial Review*, 9 Nov. 1878. The article appeared anonymously, but Howell's letter to Potter, 3 Nov. 1878, proves it was written by Howell (Letterbooks, Howell Collection, Bishopsgate Institute).

opponents of the American "caucus" eventually forced upon the parties in the United States. But, as Howell pointed out in 1878, the cost of this preliminary ballot would have nearly equalled the legal ballot at the polling booth, and, therefore, to a poor man, would have been absolutely ruinous.[1]

At that time the candidates had to pay not only their own election costs but also those of the returning officers.

That the labour leaders' concern about the "caucus" was amply justified was demonstrated by the later history of their relations, and those of their successors, with the National Liberal Federation. It was not an accident that the first Socialist organization of any significance, the Social-Democratic Federation, was originally founded as a grouping of working-class Radical clubs, designed to provide a rival focus to the National Liberal Federation. It was significant, too, that many of the working-class leaders of the Labour Party, when it came to be formed at the end of the century, were men who had been rejected as candidates by local Liberal associations—Keir Hardie at Mid-Lanark, Ramsay MacDonald at Southampton, Arthur Henderson at Newcastle.

But this is to anticipate. In the immediate situation, the National Liberal Federation did represent, for the old governing classes not used to a nation-wide participation in politics, a new and unpalatable type of organization which savoured of the methods prevalent among the pioneers of democracy, the people of the United States. It was not easy for the Radicals to maintain, after a decade of startling news about the corruption of American politics, that all was well in the Republic which they still so much admired. Nevertheless, in spite of some working-class suspicions, the old pattern of attitudes remained, with the hostility to America appearing most strongly at the top of the social scale. And so, when in the 1880 General Election the Federation proved its usefulness to the Liberal Party by inflicting a complete defeat on the Conservatives, it was naturally with the deepest distress that the Queen—confessedly no democrat—received the news from Beaconsfield that he had been worsted by "that American system called Caucus, originated by the great Radical Mr. Chamberlain."[2]

[1] *Examiner*, 26 Oct. 1878.
[2] Monypenny and Buckle, *Life of Disraeli*, vi, 535.

CHAPTER IV

THE RISE OF ECONOMIC RADICALISM AND SOCIALISM

IN 1880 the Liberal Party returned to power after a victory at the polls in which Chamberlain's Radical pressure group, the National Liberal Federation, had played a notable part.

In spite of the Queen's objections to the two Radical leaders, Joseph Chamberlain and Sir Charles Dilke, both of whom had toyed with republicanism, Gladstone took them into his ministry, the one as President of the Board of Trade, a Cabinet post, and the other as Under-Secretary for Foreign Affairs. The Radicals pressed strongly for suffrage reform, and they were assisted in some degree by the remarkable campaign waged by Andrew Carnegie, who used a portion of the profits of his Pittsburgh ironworks to purchase a number of British newspapers and to run them in the Radical interest.[1] In 1884 the Reform Bill was passed, together with a further measure for the redistribution of seats, and in the following year the Conservatives took office, Parliament was dissolved, and the new house was elected on the revised franchise, agricultural labourers voting for the first time.

At this juncture the Liberal Party ran into its gravest crisis: for the election resulted in an even balance between the Liberals on the one hand and the Conservatives and the Irish Nationalists on the other. If the Liberals were to form a new government it was essential to agree with the Irish on a plan for Home Rule for Ireland. The plan which Gladstone produced, and which Parnell accepted, failed to find favour with a large section of Gladstone's own party—a section of Whigs and very moderate Liberals led by Lord Hartington, and also a number of Radicals including Chamberlain himself and the ageing John Bright. Thus the Liberal Party was split asunder along lines which cut across previous divisions inside the party. In the ensuing confusion Gladstone, who had returned to office with the support of the

[1] Carnegie acquired no less than eighteen British newspapers. See his *Autobiography* (London, 1920), p. 330.

Irish, again dissolved Parliament, and the Liberals and Irish Nationalists, now in alliance, were soundly defeated by the Conservatives and their new allies, the dissentient Liberals or Liberal Unionists, as they came to be called. Lord Salisbury was able to form a government with the support of the Liberal Unionists, and the Liberals were to remain in opposition (except for the precarious ministry of 1892–5) for almost twenty years.

Irish Home Rule, then, was the main issue of party politics in the later eighteen-eighties: and yet there was another problem which, irrespective of constitutional struggles, kept thrusting itself into the political arena. This was the "condition of England" question, as Carlyle had called it two score years earlier, before the mid-Victorian period of comparatively steady industrial expansion had begun. By the mid-eighties, this period had been over for a dozen years; the "Great Depression" had brought chronic agricultural distress and reduced industrial profits; and cyclical unemployment at home in the later 'seventies, and again in the mid-eighties, had been matched by similar conditions in America, where measures had been taken to prevent the free influx of contract labour from Europe.[1]

It was a distressing development for the British Radicals that America was now ceasing to be the land of opportunity: for the American polity was based upon the very principles of government which they hoped to introduce into British life. If the United States had economic difficulties comparable to those of Britain, then evidently Radicalism was not enough to secure the good life. Yet there was no doubt about it: early in 1888 a leader in *Reynolds's Newspaper* sadly reported that the vices of the old country were "in a fair way of being reproduced in the new," and cited in particular the failure of the Homestead Law of 1862, on which subject the British Minister in Washington, Sir Lionel Sackville-West, had reported to the Foreign Office.[2] Industrial unemployment also became an established feature of the American scene,

---

[1] The Contract Labor laws of 1885 and 1887 were the subject of a British Home Office Circular to Mayors and Clerks of the Peace in October 1887—see *Parliamentary Papers*, 1889, lxxvi, 701.

[2] *Reynolds's Newspaper*, 8 Jan. 1888; *Parliamentary Papers*, 1887, lxxxi, 363.

and travellers who returned to England from the "Golden West" set themselves to correct the optimistic views of America held by those who had stayed at home.[1] Although emigration from Britain to the United States continued at a high level until the middle 'nineties, the total fluctuated widely in successive years in spite of the steadily improving quality of transatlantic shipping and the inexpensiveness of the journey.[2] These fluctuations seem only explicable in terms of the vicissitudes of immigrant labour in the United States. Sometimes, now, an artisan preferred to visit America for only one season of work, returning home with as much criticism as praise for the American way, and pointing out that high wages and social freedom were accompanied by long hours of work and a lack of union protection.[3]

At the same time, it was embarrassing to the Radicals to discover that the American system of government was becoming an object of friendly comment among British Conservatives, who regarded it as providing valuable safeguards against what they considered would be the evil effects of democracy. Even Lord Salisbury, who in his younger days had been one of the most violent critics of American democracy, had spoken in this sense;[4] but the best expression of the new attitude was to be found in Sir Henry Maine's *Popular Government*, the conclusion of which was that "American experience has, I think, shown that, by wise constitutional provisions thoroughly thought out beforehand, Democracy

[1] See, e.g., Morley Roberts, *The Western Avernus* (London, 1887), pp. 293 f.

[2] *Reynolds's Newspaper* in 1889 advertised passages to America at £3 10s. It has been suggested by Charlotte Erickson (*Population Studies*, iii (1949), p. 230) that an important factor in the reduction of British emigration at this time was "the rise of unions of unskilled workers and leaders who looked for improvement through Socialism." If this were true it would be difficult to explain the resumption of heavy emigration (less markedly, however, to the U.S.) in the eight years before 1914. Brinley Thomas (*Migration and Economic Growth*, pp. 108, 227) has more reasonably ascribed the fall in emigration to the switch of British investment from overseas to the home market. The fluctuations in the American demand for labour, together with the competition of other European emigrants, seem to have been the principal factors involved.

[3] *Tom Mann's Memoirs* (London, 1923), p. 33. An American consular representative in London reported in 1889 that seasonal migration of this type was still rare. *Report of Select Committee of House of Representatives to Inquire into Alleged Violation of Laws Prohibiting Immigration, etc.* (Washington, 1889), Appx.: Reports of Diplomatic and Consular Officers, p. 8.

[4] Speech reported in *The Times*, 24 Nov. 1882.

may be made tolerable."[1] The division of powers in the American constitution, and the existence of the indirectly-elected Senate and the Supreme Court were all now regarded with favour in British Conservative circles, and it was appreciated at last that the constitution created in 1787 was intended by those who framed it to be a conservative document—a point which receives almost too much emphasis in Bryce's *American Commonwealth*, and which drew upon him a reproof from the less optimistic Acton.[2]

Nevertheless, in spite of these disturbing changes there were still many Radicals who clung to the old, traditional faith in American institutions. The economy of American governmental expenditure was a strong point with them: it gave them a valuable opportunity to attack the Crown. "Gracchus," one of the columnists of *Reynolds's Newspaper*, would often argue along these lines:

> The Government of the Americans is a cheap and comparatively inexpensive one. Here we are eaten out of house and home by cats that catch no mice; there they have none of that sort. The breed, however, is greatly increasing amongst ourselves in every department of the State; and, as though we had not sufficient native paupers, the Queen is persistently increasing the number by the introduction of Germans.[3]

"Gracchus" frequently quoted with approval from Andrew Carnegie's paean of praise for his adopted country, *Triumphant Democracy* (1886)—a work which was also warmly received in the pages of the London *Democrat* and *Radical*,[4] and which sold some 40,000 copies of a British shilling edition.[5] Carnegie's opening remark that "The old nations of the earth creep on at a snail's pace; the Republic thunders past with the rush of the express" might have been expected to arouse some patriotic resentment among British readers: but many of the Radicals found in such

---

[1] H. S. Maine, *Popular Government* (London, 1885), p. 110.

[2] Acton to Bryce, n.d. (1888), Bryce Papers: "Where you speak like Macaulay speaking of 1688, I speak like Michelet speaking of 1789." For Acton's review, see *English Historical Review*, iv (1889), 388–96.

[3] *Reynolds's Newspaper*, 18 Dec. 1887.

[4] *Democrat*, 29 May 1886; *Radical*, Mar. 1887. The review in *Reynolds's Newspaper* (23 May 1886) said: "This work should be found on the shelves of every working man's library, club and institution."

[5] Burton J. Hendrick, *Life of Andrew Carnegie* (New York, 1932), i, 276.

observations only the confirmation of what they had always believed.

Furthermore, both Carnegie himself and most British Liberals and Radicals felt that the American federal system suggested the obvious solution for the principal issue of the time, Irish Home Rule.[1] Chamberlain, although hostile to Gladstone's first Home Rule proposals, which envisaged the withdrawal of Irish representation from Westminster, was at first quite willing to see some arrangement for Ireland analogous to the position of a state of the American union.[2] Gladstone later—too late—realized that a compromise with the supporters of Chamberlain might have been achieved on the lines of "the idea of the American Union":[3] too late, for Chamberlain had retreated from this position, and had begun to speak of an analogy with the constitution of Canada. *Reynolds's Newspaper* had no patience with the Canadian analogy, which it said would be opposed by "all good Radicals, whose cue it is to look to the Great Republic for their precedents, and not to the corrupt and snobbish Dominion."[4] Canada, it must be said, constantly suffered rough treatment at the hands of *Reynolds's*, which advocated its annexation by the United States on the ground that "anything that adds to the power and authority of the United States among the nations of the earth is to the advantage of all mankind."[5]

There still existed, of course, the mass of moderate Liberal opinion under Gladstone's leadership which, while critical of aspects of American life, was yet willing to regard the Republic

[1] Carnegie to Gladstone, 25 Jan. 1886, printed in Hendrick, *op. cit.*, i, 282 f. Carnegie's views carried increasing weight with the Liberals owing to the poverty of the party organization after the Home Rule split and the increasing generosity of his subventions. Hendrick, *op. cit.*, 1, 319 f.

[2] J. Chamberlain, letter to H. Labouchere, 26 Dec. 1885, printed in A. Thorold, *Life of Henry Labouchere* (London, 1913), p. 272.

[3] Gladstone Papers, B.M. Add. Mss. 44773 f. 48: Memorandum for 8 Mar. 1888. Other Liberals had of course all along been keenly alive to the American parallel, and James Bryce when editing the *Handbook of Home Rule* (London, 1887) incorporated two articles by E. L. Godkin, editor of the New York *Nation*, on this subject.

[4] *Reynolds's Newspaper*, 30 Jan. 1887.

[5] *Ibid.*, 20 Jan. 1889. This view was also held by Goldwin Smith, who was now living in Canada: *Dictionary of National Biography*, Supplement, *s.v.* "Goldwin Smith."

E

with favour rather than disfavour. For such persons, a new appraisal of the American system was sadly lacking, and in 1887 Gladstone himself deplored the fact that nothing of much consequence had been written since the work of De Tocqueville half a century before, although America itself had changed out of all recognition.[1] No one quite knew how much importance to attach to the phenomenon of American political corruption, which was now attracting much criticism from American authors. One American consul in England declared that nothing damped the enthusiasm of the English Liberal so much as the perusal of such a work as Henry Adams's *Democracy*.[2] On the other hand, Andrew Carnegie's book had skated over the subject in a way that could hardly satisfy any discerning person. The gap was fortunately filled in 1888 by James Bryce's *American Commonwealth*, which was at once acclaimed as worthy to take its place with De Tocqueville's work as a classic study of American society. Bryce, himself a prominent Liberal, did not gloss over the weaknesses which he had noticed, especially the corruption of government: but he was anxious to prevent his readers from drawing hasty conclusions from his criticism: "Few things," he wrote, "are more difficult than to use aright arguments founded on the political experience of other countries."[3] His own view was optimistic: as he said in a letter to the Cambridge philosopher Henry Sidgwick, his standpoint in the *American Commonwealth* was that

. . . altho' the U.S. is very far from being ideal, still its *social* and moral state—apart from politics—is an advance, as on the whole I think it is, on anything yet attained elsewhere.[4]

Nevertheless, as he himself anticipated, he could not prevent his work, like that of De Tocqueville, being used to justify "conclusions never intended by the author." He could not, however, claim to have been misinterpreted either by the Whig

[1] Speech opening the American Exhibition at West Brompton, reported in *The Times*, 29 Apr. 1887.

[2] *Labor in Europe*, U.S. Consular Reports, 48th Congress Ex. Doc. 54 (Washington, 1885), i, 848.

[3] *American Commonwealth* (London, 1888), i, 11.

[4] Bryce to H. Sidgwick, 4 Oct. 1888, Bryce Papers.

Edinburgh Review, which remarked sourly that he "saw American life and the American nation through rose-coloured spectacles";[1] or, on the other hand, by the Liberal *Daily News*, which, while accepting his warnings about the spoils system, the election of judges, and so on, concluded:

The best eulogy of the Americans, as we think, is that their tremendous success should render these warnings necessary. With all its drawbacks, that success is, at this day, the brightest hope of mankind. For more than a century this people has been doing what all who have ever loved their fellows have yearned to see them do, what all who have ever hated them have declared could never be done.[2]

★   ★   ★

Yet, amidst these voices which expressed, with varying degrees of knowledge and conviction, the traditional enthusiasm of the British Left for American institutions, there emerged new accents of criticism, steadily growing in volume at the end of the eighteen-eighties. This was the expression of a new generation entering politics for the first time, without the set views of the old Radicals who could remember the struggles of the Civil War and the Second Reform Act. The new generation was profoundly influenced by the propaganda of Henry George, the "prophet of San Francisco," whose book *Progress and Poverty* (1879) circulated widely on both sides of the Atlantic, and whose lecture tours in Britain in 1881–2, 1884 and 1888–9 attracted much attention.[3] What impressed the British audiences of Henry George was his insistence that there was economic distress in America which paralleled that in Britain, and which measures of constitutional reform were powerless to alleviate. As Frederic Harrison, the Positivist, said at the Industrial Remuneration Conference at Glasgow in 1885, George had

... proved, or rather directed our attention to this, viz. that the evils long familiar to all in the industrial system of Europe are already in full operation in America and other new countries.[4]

[1] *Edinburgh Review*, clxix (1889), 509.   [2] *Daily News*, 11 Dec. 1888.
[3] During the eighteen-eighties Kegan Paul sold 108,955 copies of *Progress and Poverty*; William Reeves also published a cheap edition in 1884. Elwood P. Lawrence, "Henry George's British Mission," *American Quarterly*, iii (1951), 233.
[4] *Report of the Industrial Remuneration Conference* (London, 1885), p. 429.

Many Radicals, especially the younger among them, henceforth began to turn their attention to economic affairs, though a proportion of them did not stop at George's proposed remedy for distress, which was a land tax to return the social value of the land to the community. Bernard Shaw, for instance, who attended one of George's lectures in London, later said that "He struck me dumb and shunted me from barren agnostic controversy to economics."[1] But Shaw very soon became a Socialist; and many others of those who had taken up George's views did likewise, for instance H. H. Champion, who read *Progress and Poverty* while on a visit to America in 1881, and who returned to England to become secretary of the English Land Restoration League, which was set up in 1883 for the express purpose of carrying on Georgeite propaganda. Champion however was already interested in Socialism, and in a short time he left the League to devote all his energies to building up the Social-Democratic Federation, the first of the Socialist bodies of the 1880's, of which he had become the secretary.[2] With him went J. L. Joynes, who had accompanied Henry George on a visit to Ireland in 1882. The defection of George's converts to the S.D.F., which was very tiny at this time, undoubtedly helped to establish it as a permanent organization. George himself, who was no Socialist, was naturally dismayed by the readiness of his supporters in England to go over to the Socialist ranks: but at least until 1886 there was no open acrimony between him and the Socialist leaders, either in Britain or in America, and when he fought the New York mayoralty campaign in that year he was supported by a combination of forces in which the Socialists were included. The decisive split between George and the Socialists took place as a result of the Chicago Anarchist outrage of the same year. George as a constitutionalist felt obliged to dissociate himself from the Anarchists, whom he thought had been guilty of the crime; but the Socialists both in America and Britain denounced the death sentence passed on the accused as a miscarriage of justice, and raised funds on behalf of the appeal. The case seemed particularly shocking to the British

[1] G. B. Shaw, *Sixteen Self-Sketches* (London, 1949), p. 58.
[2] For Champion's own account of this, see *Fiery Cross* (Aberdeen), 29 June 1892, a copy of which is in the John Burns Library of the T.U.C., London.

Socialists, who had previously had little conception of the harsh inefficiency of parts of the American judicial system at that time. At the height of his wrath William Morris, whose Socialist League was a semi-Anarchist secession from the Social-Democratic Federation, denounced Henry George as a "traitor";[1] and in 1889, when George spoke in London at the end of his last campaign in Britain, his remarks were interrupted with cries of "What about Chicago?"[2] The British Socialists, who religiously celebrated the anniversary of the executions of the Chicago Anarchists, liked to rub home the fact that "It was left to the country whose political institutions are the delight of so many of our Radical friends here to commit this crime."[3]

Socialism, which had been virtually non-existent in Britain in the previous decade, could not be described as a powerful political force even in the later eighteen-eighties; but several organizations had now come into existence and begun to attract national attention. Two of these have already been mentioned: the Socialist League run by William Morris, which was especially weak and soon to disintegrate; and the Social-Democratic Federation, of which Champion was secretary for a time, but which was largely controlled by H. M. Hyndman, the real pioneer of the Socialist revival in Britain. Hyndman was an educated man who had travelled widely as a journalist and company promoter and had read Marx's *Capital* in the intervals of a visit to Salt Lake City. In addition to the S.D.F. and the Socialist League, there was a small group of intellectuals who met together as the Fabian Society. Altogether, it is doubtful if the Socialist societies had as many as two thousand due-paying members between them even as late as 1889: and their importance must consequently not be over-stressed. But they were to have a major

---

[1] *Commonweal*, 12 Nov. 1887, quoted Elwood P. Lawrence, "The Uneasy Alliance: the Reception of Henry George by British Socialists in the Eighties," *American Journal of Economics and Sociology*, xi (1951–2), p. 69.

[2] *Star*, 23 May 1889. The prestige which the Anarchist cause won in British Socialist circles was probably an important factor in enabling the Anarchists to "capture" the Socialist League in 1888–90. See E. P. Thompson, *William Morris, Romantic to Revolutionary* (London, 1955), pp. 594 f.

[3] James Blackwell in *Justice*, 10 Nov. 1888. Cf. William Morris in *Signs of Change* (London, 1888), pp. 42 f.

role in determining the future of the British Left, and it is for this reason that their views are worth examining.[1]

The Socialists were obliged by their theory to find grounds for criticism in the United States, for they could not admit that political democracy was enough to make a people happy. Their predecessors earlier in the century had realized this: one of them, J. F. Bray, a Leeds compositor of American birth, was at pains to argue in his *Labour's Wrongs and Labour's Remedy* (1839) that while "the citizens of the United States . . . are exempted, by their republican form of government, from some of the grievous burthens and restrictions" imposed by the monarchical system, nevertheless America was headed for "a monarchy or an oligarchy before the end of the present century"—for "there are no greater tyrants in existence than the moneyed republicans of the United States."[2] In 1850 George Julian Harney, a Chartist leader of major importance, wrote that

A social revolution in America is a necessary and indispensable complement to the political revolution of '76. Should no such revolution, or reformation, come to pass, the future of America cannot fail to be a copy of Europe at the present time—the community divided into two great classes: a horde of brigands monopolizing all the advantages of society, and a multitude of landless profit-ridden slaves, deprived of even the name of citizens.[3]

Henry George's views, though uttered by a man who was not himself a Socialist, did much to confirm the *a priori* attitude of the Socialists to America. The words of *Progress and Poverty* seemed to disclose the beginnings of the changes that the Socialists anticipated:

The wealthy class is becoming more wealthy; but the poorer class is becoming more dependent. The gulf between the employed and the employer is growing wider; social contrasts are becoming sharper; as

---

[1] For a fuller treatment, see Henry Pelling, *Origins of the Labour Party* (London, 1954), ch. i–iv; E. P. Thompson, *op. cit.*, Part III. The Fabian Society was an offshoot of a utopian group called the Fellowship of the New Life, formed under the inspiration of Thomas Davidson of New York.

[2] J. F. Bray, *Labour's Wrongs and Labour's Remedy* (Leeds, 1839), pp. 19 f.

[3] *Red Republican*, 22 June 1850.

liveried carriages appear, so do barefoot children. . . . These are the results of private property in land.[1]

All this was grist to the Socialist mill, except for George's conclusion. For, why should one ascribe all this solely to the effect of private property in land? It was true enough that distress in America coincided with the virtual closing of the frontier, and that fortunes were made out of the steeply rising land values of the San Francisco sandlots at a time of unemployment for many of its citizens. But Britain was now an overwhelmingly industrial nation, and it was difficult to see how a tax on land values could suffice to remedy her social ills. For many British observers, the trouble was, not the monopoly of land ownership, but the concentration of ownership in industry. Yet in this respect, also, there seemed to be much to learn from America. The two decades since the end of the Civil War had seen, not only a mushroom growth of American industry, but also the aggregation of enormous industrial empires in the hands of a few leading capitalists. Such were the Carnegie steel organization, and the Standard Oil Company, and a number of the leading railway combines.

One of the first to comment on these developments in America was Henry Demarest Lloyd, himself a wealthy man, whose article "Lords of Industry" in the *North American Review* of June 1884 attracted the notice of a few of the more perceptive British Radicals. The reactions of one of the latter, the journalist William Clarke, can be seen in the correspondence which he maintained with Lloyd as a result of reading his article: in 1884 he wrote

I am troubled and saddened, to tell you the truth, by the whole course of things in America. The trading in politics and the huge growth of monopolies are portentous signs of the times. I am not going to be a reactionist, but I must confess I have had to take stock of my whole category of political beliefs and to revise my judgments.[2]

In February 1886 Clarke became formally committed to the Socialist movement by joining the Fabian Society; and in 1888, writing of the execution of the Chicago Anarchists, he told Lloyd:

[1] Henry George, *Progress and Poverty* (4th ed., New York, 1888), p. 353.
[2] Clarke to Lloyd, 22 Oct. 1884, Henry D. Lloyd Papers, Wisconsin State Historical Society.

Of course it must be expected that those who control the present social system shall avail themselves of every opportunity to crush and silence their opponents. It is really a state of *war*; and in war morality disappears.[1]

Here, then, was a Radical who, largely by studying the American scene, had reached a point of view which corresponded to the Marxist analysis of industrial society: he saw the concentration of capital and the division of society into two warring classes, which Marx had foretold, already coming to pass in the country which had been regarded as the workers' paradise. In this respect Clarke differed from Bryce, who, though aware of the trust problem, was convinced that "the struggles of labour and capital do not seem likely to take the form of a widely prevailing hatred between classes."[2]

Because of his special interest in the American scene, and his interpretation of what he saw there, Clarke's contribution to the *Fabian Essays* of 1889 was more inclined to the Marxist standpoint than were the essays of Shaw, Webb, and the others. Whereas Shaw was content to accept the views of Henry George about America, and to say that there "in confirmation of the validity of our analysis, we see all the evils of our old civilizations growing up,"[3] Clarke, quoting the evidence presented by Lloyd in "Lords of Industry," argued that America was moving ahead of Europe along a new and disastrous path—the path of industrial monopoly. Fabian gradualism would not in his view be sufficient to cope with this situation: he saw a "gulf" separating the present state of society from the Co-operative Commonwealth of the future; and along Marxist lines he anticipated the day when the people would seize control in a revolutionary act from "the weak hands of a useless possessing class."[4] This point of view was apparently accepted by only one of the other seven essayists, Hubert Bland, who was content to quote Clarke as his authority for coming to an equally Marxist conclusion:

Mr. Clarke showed us . . . that given a few more years of economic progress on present lines, and we shall reach, via the Ring and the

[1] Clarke to Lloyd, 8 Mar. 1888, Lloyd Papers.
[2] James Bryce, *American Commonwealth*, iii, 664, 668.
[3] G. B. Shaw (ed.), *Fabian Essays in Socialism* (London, 1889), p. 25.
[4] *Ibid.*, p. 101.

Trust, that period of "well-defined confrontation of rich and poor" upon which German thought has settled as the brief stage of socio-logical evolution immediately preceding organic change.[1]

Thus we find, embedded in the *Fabian Essays* which for over half a century were to form the basis of British Socialist thought, a Marxist interpretation of social evolution founded upon an analysis of American industrial society; while the major thesis of gradualism to be found in most of the essays is linked with the milder assumption that conditions in America, if no worse than elsewhere, were nevertheless approaching the European norm of social injustice.[2]

Although most Socialists accepted the growth of trusts in America as a confirmation of the Marxist interpretation, their reactions varied from the pessimism of the Anti-State Socialists, who regarded the concentration of industry as a serious problem, to the optimism of the State Socialists who considered that it would facilitate the concentration of control which they favoured. The latter view was taken by the American writer Edward Bellamy, whose vision of the future, entitled *Looking Backward, 2000–1887*, circulated widely on both sides of the Atlantic towards the end of the decade. The book forecast the growth of vast industrial aggregations which would pass readily from private to public hands. It was reviewed favourably by the secretary of the S.D.F., H. W. Lee, in *Justice*, the party organ:[3] but the more anarchistic William Morris, who at this time was loud in the denunciation of the "American spirit,"[4] criticized the "machine life" that Bellamy envisaged and the "economic semi-fatalism" which was expected to bring about his ideal.[5] Morris wrote his *News from Nowhere* to depict an alternative ideal—a society in which both state control and large-scale industry had been banished from the scene.

[1] *Fabian Essays in Socialism*, p. 202.
[2] Gaylord Wilshire, the American Socialist, who was in England at this time, later recalled the refusal of Shaw to believe that America was industrially in advance of Europe, and that "it was this superiority of America which had caused the trust." *Socialism Inevitable* (New York, 1906), p. 199.
[3] *Justice*, 16 Mar. 1889.
[4] Clarke to Lloyd, 9 Dec. 1889, recounting a recent conversation with Morris, Lloyd Papers.
[5] *Commonweal*, 22 June 1889.

Naturally Hyndman was in sympathy with the interpretation of his colleague Lee rather than with that of Morris, and he hailed the trusts as convincing evidence of the way events were preparing for an early revolution. He also regarded them as an indication that the mild medicine of a tax on land would not suffice to remedy social ills. Thus in 1889, when he engaged in a public debate with Henry George on the subject of "The Single Tax versus Socialism," he could point to the marked development of industrial monopoly in the United States.[1] Hyndman also regarded it as valuable that these economic changes were acting as a stimulus for the growth of a revolutionary movement inside the United States. In 1886 he wrote an article, which was at once published as a pamphlet, on "The Chicago Riots and the Class War in the United States"; and in it he declared that

The corruption of the state legislatures and the municipalities, the hopelessness of getting any matters attended to which affect the welfare of great masses of men, but which conflict with the interests of the great monopolies, are steadily driving the intelligent workers to the conviction that, if the present attitude is maintained, an appeal to downright force is the only solution of the question.

Hyndman claimed to have noticed on every visit to America since 1870 an "increasing difficulty for a man to rise out of the wage-earning classes," and argued that the relations of employer and employed were characterized by an even more unpleasant "cold, pecuniary bargain" than in Europe. The situation was aggravated, in Hyndman's opinion, by the willingness of Americans to resort to arms against each other.[2]

A similar view was taken by Friedrich Engels, who surveyed the world development of Socialism from his home on Primrose Hill in London. Engels greeted with special enthusiasm the "United Labor Party" that grew up to support Henry George's mayoralty campaign and to fight other electoral battles. Writing at the peak of this movement, and at a time when the Knights of Labor had secured their maximum strength of about 700,000 members, Engels spoke of "the favoured soil of America, where no medieval

---

[1] See verbatim report of the debate, *Single Tax versus Socialism* (London, 1889), esp. p. 12.

[2] *Time*, n.s., iii (1886), p. 698.

ruins bar the way, where history begins with the elements of modern bourgeois society."[1] Engels encouraged Marx's daughter Eleanor and her husband Edward Aveling to visit America to see for themselves, and they wrote on their return:

The example of the American working man will be followed before long on the European side of the Atlantic. An English, or, if you will, a British Labour Party will be formed. . . .[2]

Nor were these hopes limited to the Marxists. *Reynolds's* in 1887 directed the attention of the British workers to what it significantly called "the latest development of labour politics in the Greater Britain of the United States." The same article concluded that "The makeshift rule of thumb economics of Trades Unionism are simply a disgrace to British workmen, and the sooner they take a leaf out of the book of their American brethren the better."[3] A few weeks later, it was suggested that the Labour Electoral Association which the T.U.C. had brought into existence might model itself upon the pattern of the American United Labour Party.[4]

These years at the end of the eighteen-eighties constitute one of the few periods when the state of political organization of the working class as such in America could be regarded as more complete than that of the British workers. The Knights of Labor provided a remarkable example in the unionization of the unskilled, at a time when the "new unions" had not yet come into existence in Britain. One of *Reynolds's* commentators, "Demos," suggested to the Irish labour leader Michael Davitt in an open letter that he should take the lead in the work of organizing the unskilled, many of whom were Irishmen, along the lines of the Knights of Labor:[5] and in the following year Davitt, who had visited America and attended a convention of the Knights at Minneapolis, took the hint and spoke at a meeting in Smethwick

[1] F. Engels, *Condition of the Working Class in England in 1844* (New York, 1887), p. ii (preface dated Jan. 1887).
[2] E. & E. Marx Aveling, *Working Class Movement in America* (London, 1887), pp. 152 f.
[3] *Reynolds's Newspaper*, 11 Sept. 1887.   [4] *Ibid.*, 25 Sept. 1887.
[5] *Ibid.*, 10 July 1887. "Demos" at this time may have been the young W. M. Thompson, who became editor on the death of the founder's brother in 1894. Thompson was friendly to the Socialists and much influenced by them.

to spread the Order in Britain.[1] How many workers actually joined the British Assemblies of the Knights is not known, but although the Order never established itself on a permanent basis in Britain it is probable that the total of those who belonged at one time or another ran into five figures.[2] Bellamy's Nationalist movement, which owed its origin to the favourable reception of his book *Looking Backward*, also spread to Britain, where a Nationalization of Labour Society was set up with several branches and a journal called the *Nationalization News*. Another American Socialist author, Laurence Gronlund, became quite well-known in England, his work *The Co-operative Commonwealth* being published in London in two editions, the second of which was edited by Bernard Shaw.[3] All these developments showed that at the time the interest in Socialism and "advanced" labour movements was at least as great in America as in Britain, and that new initiatives in this field often came to Britain from across the Atlantic. It was in these years that Jim Connell wrote the "Red Flag" with its reference to American Socialism, "Chicago swells the surging throng."[4] Engels thought in 1888 that

The two great Anglo-Saxon countries are sure to get up competition in Socialism, as well as in all other things, and then it will be a race with ever-accelerated velocity.[5]

This prophecy, indeed, was not to be fulfilled: but its failure could not readily be discerned for many years to come.

★ ★ ★

Thus, while moderate Liberals and old-fashioned Radicals were still savouring the advantages of the American political structure—

[1] *Star*, 14 May 1888; see also J. Chapman to T. V. Powderly, 3 Mar. 1888, Knights of Labor Papers, Catholic University of America, Washington, D.C.

[2] For a fuller treatment of this topic see Henry Pelling, "Knights of Labor in Britain, 1880–1901," to be published in the *Economic History Review*.

[3] Gronlund also came to England in 1885 and took part in the work of the Socialist League. See Glasier's reminiscence in *Labour Leader*, 2 Dec. 1905. I owe this reference to Mr. C. Tsuzuki.

[4] The "Red Flag" was first published in *Justice*, 21 Dec. 1889. Even the choice of May Day for special celebration by the Second International owes much to an American initiative—see Sidney Fine, "Is May Day American in Origin?", *Historian*, xvi (1954), pp. 121–34.

[5] Engels to Mrs. Wischnewetzky, 22 Feb. 1888, printed in K. Marx and F. Engels, *Letters to Americans, 1848–1895* (New York, 1953), p. 197.

the former sometimes noticing with approval certain restrictions on the excess of democracy which they had not seen before—those who were concerned especially about economic inequality and distress made the discovery, for the first time, that America was in a similar case with Britain in this respect. Unemployment and poverty on the one hand, and the growth of monopoly on the other, were now prominent features of the American scene: and these features stimulated the conversion of British Radicals to a Socialist or Socialistic standpoint. William Clarke in the middle of the 'nineties lucidly described this process of conversion to Socialism which he and many others of the younger Radicals had undergone:

A quarter of a century ago the American Republic was the guiding star of advanced English political thought. It is not so now; candour compels me to say that. It is not merely a question of machine politics, of political corruption, of the omnipotent party boss. . . . Over and beyond this is the great fact of the division between rich and poor, millionaires at one end, tramps at the other, a growth of monopolies unparalleled, crises producing abject poverty just as in Europe. These facts proved to men clearly that new institutions were of no use along with the old forms of property; that a mere theoretic democracy, unaccompanied by any social changes, was a delusion and a snare.[1]

In these words Clarke summed up the rapid crystallization of a new attitude to America on the part of the younger members of the Left: an attitude that was to develop and flourish for many years to come.

[1] W. Clarke, "The Fabian Society," in *Fabian Essays in Socialism* (American ed., reprinted Boston, Mass., 1908), p. xxi.

CHAPTER V

THE AMERICAN ECONOMY
AND THE FOUNDATION OF
THE LABOUR PARTY

IN 1900 an important group of British trade union leaders took the important step—in association with and largely at the instigation of the Socialists—of founding a political party of their own. This was the inception of the Labour Party, which after a shaky start eventually displaced the Liberal Party as one of the two main British political organizations. The trade union members of the Labour Party, or the Labour Representation Committee (L.R.C.) as it was known until the 1906 General Election, were usually Liberal rather than Socialist in general political standpoint, and many differences of political outlook separated them from their Socialist colleagues. The main Socialist body was now the Independent Labour Party (I.L.P.), founded in 1893, which was both less Marxist in tone and more working-class in leadership than Hyndman's S.D.F.: its leaders had played a key role in the formation of the L.R.C., and one of its members, Ramsay MacDonald, was the first L.R.C. secretary. But even the reformist Socialists of the I.L.P. often found themselves at odds with the Liberal trade union leadership. One important common attitude, however, had helped to forge the alliance of trade unionist and Socialist, and proved of value in solidifying it: all were motivated by a common concern for the future of the industrial worker in what seemed to be a rapidly changing economic system. In these years at the turn of the century, the trade union leaders who supported the Labour Representation Committee did so in the belief that the trust system already prevalent in America was going to spread to Britain; that these trusts, using the unscrupulous methods that were regarded as normal in American labour relations, would be able seriously to damage the British trade union movement: and that the only way to avoid this would be to elect a large group of independent labour representatives to

Parliament. The present chapter is devoted to a study of the nature of this interest in American industrial developments.

★   ★   ★

Already in the eighteen-eighties, as we have seen, the phenomenon of the American trusts had aroused interest among a limited number of British political writers and economists. In the early 'nineties, however, this interest did not seem to develop. Lloyd's powerful study of the Standard Oil Trust, *Wealth against Commonwealth* (1894), occasioned little immediate stir in Britain, and at first it was only the prominent Socialists, such as H. M. Hyndman and the I.L.P. leader Keir Hardie, and the keenest students of American affairs, such as Bryce, J. A. Hobson, and the journalist W. T. Stead, who regarded the work as being of primary significance.[1] It was not until 1897 that British labour leaders in general began to study the details of American industrial organization. In the latter part of that year they underwent the chastening experience of a six months' struggle in the British engineering industry which ended in the defeat of the union. It was the first strike or lock-out ever to develop into a nation-wide conflict, and this novel feature was due to the recent formation of a national Engineering Employers' Federation. Although the Federation was not in any sense a trust, it was a form of association which undoubtedly strengthened the hands of the employers in

[1] For appreciative letters to Lloyd from British readers, see the Henry D. Lloyd Papers in the Wisconsin State Historical Society. Hobson regarded it as "the most powerful and convincing exposure of the natural working of developed Capitalism that has appeared" (Hobson to Lloyd, 22 Feb. 1895). A later reaction, from Bruce Glasier, Hardie's friend and successor as chairman of the I.L.P., is of interest in showing the various impressions of America that conflicted in the mind of the moderate Socialist in Britain: "One can hardly believe that such things could be possible in a land from which so many of us have derived so much of the most exalted conception of human achievement. For in the literature of America there is a quality of the very highest and rarest nobility and tenderness that has yet been given to us. And when one thinks that future historians of our period will have to include side by side with the writings of Emerson, Whitman, Whittier, Lowell and Burroughs . . . the villainies of the Goulds, Vanderbilts, Rockefellers and Carnegies, one marvels at the inscrutable problem of 'Culture and Anarchy' which they will have set before them" (Glasier to Lloyd, 20 Oct. 1897).

dealing with the unions; and, taken in conjunction with the *obiter dicta* of the leaders of the Federation during the struggle, it seemed to show that Britain was likely to follow the path of industrial change on the American pattern.

Further developments of the trust system in the United States rapidly took place in the immediately following years: a large number of important fresh amalgamations were made, frequently under the cover of the comparatively lax corporation laws of New Jersey. The process culminated in 1901 with the formation of the United States Steel Corporation, which united the interests of Pierpont Morgan, Carnegie and others in a vast new trust with a share capital of over a billion dollars.[1]

The world-wide significance of these industrial changes was not at first brought home to the British public. The occasional British visitor in America might be shocked, as was G. W. Steevens, the *Daily Mail* correspondent, into describing the trusts as "a return to savagery" and "the tyrants of the whole community."[2] But the real impact on British public opinion was not made until the trusts "invaded" the British shipping and tobacco industries. In May 1901 Morgan purchased control of the shipping line of Frederick Leyland & Co., and in April 1902 he also acquired the White Star Line. The new company, known as the International Mercantile Marine Company, was heavily over-capitalized, the British interests having been obtained at an inflated price, and it seemed hardly possible that it could justify itself financially except by controlling and raising transatlantic rates. But what really alarmed British opinion was the knowledge that a substantial part of the shipping industry, which was of the greatest strategic importance to the country, could be transferred to foreign hands by a stroke of the pen.[3] Equally perturbing in its implications, if not for its own sake, was the acquisition of Ogdens Ltd., the tobacco firm, by the American Tobacco Company in September 1901. This was met by prompt resistance on the part of the re-

---

[1] Eliot Jones, *The Trust Problem in the United States* (New York, 1921), pp. 40–3.

[2] G. W. Steevens, *Land of the Dollar* (Edinburgh, 1897), pp. 306 f.

[3] See the Commons debate on "The Transatlantic Shipping Combine," 1 May 1902, in which Bryce took part (*Parl. Deb.*, 4th ser., cvii, 457–94).

maining British tobacco firms, eleven of which at once pooled their assets into the Imperial Tobacco Company, and in 1902 waged a brisk sales war against the American intruders, forcing them to come to terms which involved the return of Ogdens to British control.[1]

These events caused concern among people of all shades of political opinion in Britain. The horror of the outraged patriot and the dismay of the threatened capitalist were matched by the gloomy forebodings of political Radicals and labour leaders at the emergence of a financial oligarchy of world power, based on the United States. Optimism about the situation was almost entirely confined to the Marxian Socialists such as Hyndman, who thought that "these trusts will bring us Socialism quickly":[2] but even they accepted the view that things would be worse before they were better.

A correspondent of the Liberal *Daily News* voiced a not untypical reaction when he wrote:

The present crisis has arisen because the Americans, following methods which admit of no moral sanction, are deliberately striking a blow at the very foundations of British prosperity, and are forcing British captains of industry in self-defence to resort, not only to the latest machinery, but to the latest extravagance of commercial tyranny.[3]

[1] H. W. Macrosty, *Trust Movement in British Industry* (London, 1907), pp. 229–36, 301–6.

[2] Hyndman to Henry Demarest Lloyd, 19 Apr. 1901 (Henry D. Lloyd Papers). Cf. A. P. Hazell, another S.D.F. member, in *London Trades and Labour Gazette*, June 1902. Curiously, Sir Charles Dilke is to be ranked with the Marxians on this issue: "I am rather inclined . . . to agree with those Socialists who think that the marked tendency toward the control of great enterprises by a few hands helps toward that municipalization of some and that nationalization of others which personally I favour."—Dilke to H. G. Wilshire, 29 May 1902, published in *Wilshire's Magazine* (Toronto, Canada), Aug. 1902.

[3] *Daily News*, 5 Apr. 1902, "The Peril of Trusts," by a Correspondent. Apart from Dilke, the principal exception to the prevailing pessimism in the Radical ranks was W. T. Stead, whose remarkable forecast *The Americanization of the World* was published as the 1902 annual of the *Review of Reviews* which he edited. Frederic Whyte's *Life of W. T. Stead* (London, 1925) does not deal adequately with Stead's various interests in the American scene: but for all his power as a journalist he was a political eccentric. See his *If Christ Came to Chicago* (1894), *Chicago Today* (1894), *Satan's Invisible World Displayed: or Despairing Democracy* (1897) and *Mr. Carnegie's Conundrum* (1898). Whyte deals with his relations with Cecil Rhodes; but he was also much influenced by Carnegie, for which see the Carnegie Papers, Library of Congress, Washington, D.C., notably Carnegie to Stead, 10 Jan. 1902.

F

Among those most affected by the prevailing alarm were the British trade union leaders. When they looked at the transatlantic scene, they were reminded of the weakness of the American unions in comparison with their own. In 1897 the membership of the American Federation of Labor was only 265,000 as against the T.U.C. figure of 1,093,000; and although the American total rapidly increased in the following seven years to a peak of 1,676,000 in 1904, the A.F.L. was still little larger than the T.U.C. (which had also grown considerably) and in proportion to the total population of the respective countries American unionism was only half as successful as British.[1] It was a matter of grave concern to the unionists that their movement should be so weak in the country which appeared to have the most highly developed forms of industrial organization.

There was another fact, too, which made the union leaders anxious about the state of things in America. The employers in Britain had developed the habit of arguing that it was the freedom of American industry from the restrictions of trade unionism that accounted for its competitive advantage.[2] Thus, during the Engineers' lock-out of 1897 Colonel Dyer, the employers' leader, who had visited and admired the Carnegie works at Pittsburgh, declared that the object of the Engineering Employers' Federation was

to obtain the freedom to manage their own affairs which has proved so beneficial to the American manufacturers as to enable them to compete . . . in what was formerly an English monopoly.[3]

This argument was elaborated in a *Times* article on "The Engineering Industry in England and America," which took the form of an interview with an unnamed American manufacturer. The American was quoted as saying that the superiority of industry

---

[1] S. Perlman and P. Taft, *History of Labour in the United States, 1896–1932*, iv (New York, 1935), p. 13; G. D. H. Cole, *Short History of the British Working-Class Movement* (London 1948), pp. 275, 484.

[2] "They [the employers] are everlastingly quoting the practice of America, and declaring that in America there is no attempt of any kind made by the men to regulate the speed of machines or objection raised by them as to the number of machines any man shall work." Tom Mann, in a letter published in the *American Federationist* (organ of the A.F.L.), Dec. 1897.

[3] *The Times*, 7 Sept. 1897.

in his country was due to the lack of interference from trade unions; his view of the continuing lock-out in Britain was that "if the men persist in what they are doing they will drive the engineering industry proper out of England."[1]

These utterances made the union leaders all the more ready to believe the worst of American labour conditions. G. N. Barnes, the secretary of the Amalgamated Society of Engineers, who was himself a member of the I.L.P., in a reply to Colonel Dyer spoke bitterly of the Carnegie Company's 1892 strike at Homestead,

. . . when armed men were retained to shoot down workmen, when the works were encircled by barbed wire and explosives, and a condition of things brought about which bordered on civil war. We venture to think that the enlightened public opinion of this country would resent the introduction here of the "Boss" system, with its attendant unrestrained brutality and lawlessness.[2]

The Pullman strike of 1894, the union leaders recalled, had witnessed not only violence of the same sort, but also an unprecedented extension of the use of legal injunctions to prevent picketing. This weapon was primarily responsible for the failure of the American Railway Union, whose leader, Eugene V. Debs, was sent to prison.

Although the possibilities of violence in British industrial conflicts seemed to have increased in recent years in England, owing to the formation in 1893 of the "National Free Labour Association" for the supply of blackleg workers, it was not so much the direct attack on their rights by force or the threat of force that the trade union leaders feared, but rather the indirect strategy of encroachment on their rights by judicial decision on the pattern of the Debs case in America. The legal systems of England and America were closely akin, both being founded upon the common law, and although the British unions had for some time considered themselves to be well protected by the legislation of 1871–6, they had recently had occasion for some concern. A number of members of the Royal Commision on Labour (1891–4) had recommended changes in the legal status of the unions,[3] and if the employers' counter-attack developed with the general

---

[1] *The Times*, 23 Sept. 1897. [2] *Ibid.*, 9 Sept. 1897.
[3] Final Report of the Royal Commission on Labour (*Parliamentary Papers*, 1894, xxxv), pp. 115–19.

support of middle-class opinion, there was no knowing what might happen. In the course of the Engineers' lock-out Henry Demarest Lloyd, who was then on a visit to England, had issued a warning to the effect that British lawyers were studying American methods of dealing with labour troubles;[1] and several test cases had already arisen to indicate that, to say the least, the judges had a remarkably large area for manoeuvre in the interpretation of existing statutes.[2]

At the same time the employers' point of view on the damaging effects of trade unionism continued to obtain wide publicity. The industrial correspondent of *The Times*, Edwin A. Pratt, was fully in sympathy with them, and in 1900 he arranged a series of articles on the subject of "American Engineering Competition," two of which dealt with the labour problem.[3] The principal finding of these articles was declared as follows:

> If there is one thing more plainly revealed than another by being brought into contact with American engineering factories . . . it is that the rule of militant trade unionism must be broken. . . . Militant trade unions have been the chief means of stopping the advance of British engineering industry, and in the interests of the men, as well as of the rest of the nation, their unreasonable and pernicious rule must be suppressed.

The articles maintained that the unions were responsible for holding back the development of the industry, not only by pressing for unreasonably high wages and short hours, but also by employing restrictive practices such as insistence on the engagement of skilled men for unskilled jobs, and opposition to the introduction of labour-saving machinery.[4]

[1] *New Age*, 28 Nov. 1897. That there was some truth in the warning may be seen from the citation of American cases in W. J. Shaxby, *The Case Against Picketing* (4th ed., London, 1900). Shaxby was assistant secretary of the Liberty and Property Defence League.

[2] The most important cases were *Allen* v. *Flood* and *Lyons* v. *Wilkins*. See *Law Reports* (1899), 1 Ch. 255 and (1898) A.C.1.

[3] *The Times*, 13 June and 10 July 1900. The articles were however criticized on technical grounds. See *Iron and Coal Trades Review*, 16 Nov. 1900, p. 1006.

[4] The charges were repeated in America and caused Samuel Gompers, the President of the A.F.L., to write to several British union leaders for a reasoned refutation which he could use. See Gompers to E. Cowey, etc., 3 June 1901, in Gompers Letter-books, A.F.L., Washington D.C. For the replies, see *American Federationist*, Sept. 1901, pp. 351 ff.

The attitude of *The Times* showed little detachment from the current controversies between capital and labour.[1] It leant heavily in the direction of the views of the more uncompromising employers. Indeed, it seems clear that on this subject there was a close collaboration between *The Times* and some of the members of the British Iron Trade Association, one of whom, H. J. Skelton, a Sheffield steel merchant, in the course of a lecture at the Association's annual conference quoted extensively from a *Times* leader in support of the view that Americans developed the "individuality" of their workmen "which declines to sink itself in the monotony of mediocrity encouraged by English trade unions."[2]

There is no reason to suppose that very many trade unionists read *The Times*, but their official leaders attached great importance to its influence in the shaping of public opinion. *The Times* attacks, coinciding as they did with what the union leaders regarded as infringements of their rights under the Trade Union Acts, increased their already mounting concern about the American experience—concern which reached a climax with the decision of the vitally important Taff Vale case. In the summer of 1900 the employees of the Taff Vale Railway Company went on strike, and following the precedent of the Pullman strike in America the

---

[1] For a valuable contemporary examination, in detail, of *The Times* charges, see P. Mantoux and M. Alfassa, *La Crise du Trade-Unionisme* (Paris, 1903). The authors had no difficulty in showing the distortions involved in the charges. The *Daily Chronicle* was much more sensible: see the leader of 16 Nov. 1901.

[2] *Iron and Coal Trades Review*, 15 June 1900; *The Times*, 19 Apr. 1900 (for the leader). A similar point of view is to be found in J. S. Jeans (ed.), *American Industrial Conditions and Competition*: Reports of the Commissioners appointed by the British Iron Trade Association (London, 1902), esp. p. 318. This work is criticized in *Amalgamated Engineers Journal*, Aug. 1902, under the heading "Americanism." A more balanced view of the whole controversy is to be found in "Regulation and Restriction of Output in Great Britain," *Eleventh Special Report of the Commissioner of Labor* (Washington D.C., 1904), esp. pp. 721 f. and 736 ("Origin of Ca'Canny"). See also A. Maurice Low, "Labor Unions and British Industry," *Bulletin of the Bureau of Labor*, No. 50 (Jan. 1904). The organ of the British textile employers attributed the troubles of their own industry to the alleged fact that "in not a single establishment manned by trade-union workers is the production more than two-thirds of what it ought to be," whereas "the methods of battling trade-unionism have been reduced to a science in the United States and their adoption seems to be uniformly successful."—*Textile Mercury*, 24 Aug. 1901. I owe this reference to Mr. Frank Bealey.

company sought an injunction against the Amalgamated Society of Railway Servants, to which the strikers belonged. To the dismay of the Society, and to the general consternation of the whole trade union movement, the injunction was upheld in the High Court. This was in September 1900. In the Court of Appeal the decision was reversed, but the case was taken to the House of Lords, and there, in July 1901, the final decision went once more against the union. In August, a second important case involving the Trade Union Acts, *Quinn* v. *Leathem*, was also decided by the Lords against the union concerned.[1]

While the cases were *sub judice* the employers' position received steady support from *The Times*, whose industrial correspondent Pratt was preparing a series of articles from his own pen on what he chose to call "The Crisis in British Industry." The articles, which were published between November 1901 and January 1902, surveyed labour problems in a wide range of trades, and bitterly criticized the union for "ca'canny" or go-slow tactics and restrictive practices.[2] The bricklayers came in for especially harsh criticism because of an alleged union limitation on the number of bricks laid by each man per day.[3] While little direct evidence was provided, the impression was effectively conveyed that the unions were responsible for seriously hampering the development of British industrial productivity and ability to compete in the world market. This impression was heightened by the numerous letters on the subject which *The Times* published. Other newspapers took up the controversy, mostly siding with *The Times*: the *Daily Mail*, for instance, secured a further count against the trade unions by interviewing Charles Schwab, the President of the steel trust, in the course of his visit to England. Schwab was reported as saying:

You ask me what reasons I can give for the superiority of American over British labour? Undoubtedly trade unionism. In England these

[1] *Law Reports* (1901), A.C. 426 and 495.
[2] Republished later as a book, E. A. Pratt, *Trade Unionism and British Industry* (London, 1904).
[3] These criticisms had already been rehearsed by William Woodward, an architect, in "The British Workman and His Competitors," *Nineteenth Century*, xlix (March, 1901), pp. 456–60.

corporations proceed upon utterly fallacious principles. Trade unionism in England takes away all the enthusiasm of individual effort.[1]

Finally, the argument was carried into Parliament in the course of a debate which arose from the Taff Vale decision. On 14 May 1902, Mr. C. B. Renshaw, Conservative M.P. for West Renfrewshire and head of a firm of carpet manufacturers, made the principal speech against a proposal to pass special legislation to protect the unions. In the course of his remarks he made the following point:

> In many of the great industrial works in America there is far greater freedom in regard to the exercise of the powers of the industrial workman in his work to do a larger amount of work, and to be progressive in the character of his work, than is permitted to a workman in this country under the rules and regulations of trade unions.[2]

How did the trade union leaders react to this barrage of damaging charges? Sensitive as they were to changes in public opinion, they knew that they could not ignore the attacks. They naturally hastened to deny that the activities of the unions limited the competitive strength of British industry. The Amalgamated Society of Engineers, because of its struggle for shorter hours in 1897, had already been obliged to defend itself on this score at the bar of public opinion. G. N. Barnes, the union's general secretary, had ably expounded its case in a "Manifesto to the Public" in July of that year. The British industry, he said, had beaten its competitors in the past in spite of relatively high wages and short hours; and he maintained that

> . . . the probable source of foreign competition, if any, will come, if at all, from the highly specialized, sub-divided and highly-paid American centres.[3]

[1] *Daily Mail*, 15 Jan. 1902.

[2] *Parliamentary Debates*, 4th ser., cviii, 303. For further discussion in 1902 involving criticism of the unions, see Sir Christopher Furness, M.P., "The Old World and the American Invasion," *Pall Mall Magazine*, xxvi, 362–8; A. Montefiore-Brice, "Trade-Unions and National Welfare," *Temple Bar*, cxxv, 399–414; J. Holt Schooling, "Letter Addressed to the Workmen of the United Kingdom," *Fortnightly Review*, n.s. lxxii, 480–3; B. H. Thwaite, *The American Invasion* (London, 1902), pp. 16–19. A view more favourable to British labour is to be found in F. A. McKenzie, *The American Invaders* (London, 1902), ch. xx.

[3] Amalgamated Society of Engineers, "First Manifesto to the Public," 12 July 1897, reprinted in *id.*, *Notes on the Engineering Trades Lock-out* (London, 1898), appx. p. 31.

Barnes was not speaking from personal experience of American conditions, for he had not at that time visited America; but his union received a good deal of information about American engineering conditions, as it had branches in the United States and many of its members had worked in America for at least a season. Barnes was supported by John Burns, M.P., a member of his Executive, who had lately visited America on a fraternal visit to the A.F.L.:

The real test of effective industrial competition is not hours worked or wages paid: the determining factor is the cost per ton, the price per horse-power, and invariably the most successful competitor is he who harnesses short hours and high wages to skilled supervision, good design, economic working, utilitarian and varying demand of customer.

And Burns went on to contrast the obsolete equipment and methods of many British firms with the efficiency of Brown and Sharpe's, Rhode Island, and Brotherhood's of Lambeth.[1]

The reply to the more generalized attacks of later years was made on similar lines. The Management Committee of the General Federation of Trade Unions replied promptly to the early articles of *The Times* series on "The Crisis in British Industry." They refuted the charge of "ca'canny" practices and then proceeded to argue that a high-wage industry was kept up-to-date by the very fact of having high labour costs. Thus, by contrast with the languishing state of agriculture, whose labour force was both unorganized and miserably paid,

. . . in such trades as engineering, shipbuilding, mining, etc., Labour has by organization won for itself better conditions in regard to wages and hours, which betterment has led to the stimulation of invention and the introduction of machinery with immense advantage to all engaged as well as to the community. The statement, therefore, that the unions have prevented the introduction of labour-saving machinery or appliances is not only not true, but absolutely the reverse of the truth.[2]

Undoubtedly there was a strong case for the view that a high-wage economy stimulated inventiveness and provided many competitive advantages. Not only trade unionists, but also

---

[1] *The Times*, 27 Sept. 1897.   [2] *Ibid.*, 20 Dec. 1901.

progressive employers like W. H. Lever the soap manufacturer had pointed this out.[1] The defence of the trade unions against a general charge of restrictive practices was, however, a little more difficult, especially in the face of the constantly multiplying accusations that were contained in the letters published by *The Times*. The most authoritative rebuttal came from Sidney and Beatrice Webb, the historians of the movement. The Webbs maintained that the unionist was a better worker than the non-unionist, and that although the instinctive reaction of the worker was to adopt restrictive practices in some form in order to protect his job and status, nevertheless this instinct was discouraged by the union leadership. *The Times* articles, said the Webbs, were "a torrent of indiscriminate abuse" which "does not encourage the party of progress within the trade-union movement."[2] The Webbs made no reference to the situation in America, and this was subsequently dealt with by Clement Edwards, a former trade union official who had become a barrister and who appeared for the Railway Servants in the Taff Vale case. Edwards, in an article in the *Contemporary Review*, maintained that "ca'canny" was, first of all, very rare in Britain, and, secondly, quite as common in America. Strikes on "the question of mechanical appliances" were common to both the British and the American boot and shoe industries, though the object of the workers in both countries was not to prevent the introduction of machinery but simply to get better pay if the work was speeded up. English workmen, in fact, according to Edwards, were actually less unreasonable about new machinery than were German or American workmen.[3]

Such was the immediate defence of trade union leaders and their sympathizers in the journals of upper- and middle-class opinion. In the labour and left-wing press, however, the general alarm had set on foot a formidable counter-attack. Did the employers find conditions better for their own class in America? Then they must be worse for the workers. It had been widely accepted in Britain that the growth of the trusts was having an

[1] *New Liberal Review*, i (March 1901), 260.   [2] *The Times*, 6 Dec. 1901.
[3] Clement Edwards, "Do Trade Unions Limit Output?", *Contemporary Review*, lxxxi (Jan. 1902), 113–28. Edwards had at one time been assistant secretary of the London Dockers—see *Labour Annual*, 1895, p. 168. In 1906 he became a Liberal M.P.

adverse effect on the position of American trade unionism. This view was, of course, sedulously fostered by the Socialists, who believed that the concentration of capital would inevitably be accompanied by the increasing misery of the workers, as Marx had forecast. The pages of the Socialist papers, and especially of the S.D.F. weekly *Justice*, were full of assertions to this effect.[1] But in any case there could be no doubt that American unionism was weaker than that of Britain, where the processes of industrial concentration had not advanced so fast or so far. It was not difficult to ignore the other factors that accounted for the weakness of American unionism, such as the heterogeneity of the population, the heavy rate of immigration, and the problems of organization presented in so vast a country. American trade unionists, naturally, had much to say in denunciation of the trusts and their attitude to the unions. Thus, for instance, E. F. O'Rourke, a fraternal delegate of the A.F.L. to the 1901 Trades Union Congress, said of the strike then current in the steel industry that

Victory for the Trust would mean the death of organized labour in the United States. . . . The Trust was endeavouring to destroy trade unionism.[2]

And Isaac Cowen, the general organizer of the American branches of the Engineers, wrote bitterly to London in January 1901:

America has had the advantage of the skill and ingenuity of men from all nations of the world, who have come here to seek a home. . . . As a rule, the Rockefellers, Morgans, Vanderbilts, Carnegies and other trust magnates have captured these benefits for themselves, either through prostrated courts, bribed legislators, or using the gatling gun wherever organized labor demanded a small portion of their product.[3]

---

[1] Thus Hyndman reported in *Justice*, 2 Dec. 1899: "At present unions had succeeded in heading back the American system of driving, but even on this point the general economic advance was against them. Machinery was being speeded here to the same rate as over the water. . . . Combinations of employers were progressing rapidly. So were trusts, and employers meant to weaken the influence of trade unionism."

[2] T.U.C. *Report*, 1901, p. 59. O'Rourke's contention was not greatly exaggerated: Perlman and Taft in their *History of Labor in the U.S.*, iv, 57 ff., describe the steel strike as "Labor's Defeat at the Marne."

[3] *Amalgamated Engineers Journal*, Mar. 1901, pp. 19 f.

British observers were impressed with the violence that sometimes accompanied strikes in America, and this phenomenon was also regarded as primarily a product of the new industrial system, although much of it was due to the special features of American life which have been mentioned as largely responsible for the weakness of the unions. In general, the further west, the more violence there was: in the mining regions of the Rocky Mountains the "characteristics of the frontier"[1] were undoubtedly the determining factor. But this was not obvious to the British union leader, who surveyed the American scene from a distance. Barnes's remark during the 1897 Engineers' struggle has already been quoted: it was natural for him to associate the "unrestrained brutality and lawlessness" of American strikes with what he called the "boss system" of factory management.

It was somewhat embarrassing for British union leaders to have to admit that in spite of the weakness of the American unions, rates of wages were much higher in American industry than in British. The difference in the cost of living was not sufficient to account for this. The only solution was to suggest that conditions of work in America were bad, and the hours excessively long. Barnes, who had conducted the 1897 struggle of the Engineers principally with the object of winning the eight-hour day, was emphatic that only shorter hours would allow the workers time for self-education, and that education was essential, not only for the well-being of the worker, but also for the progress of industry.[2] In the course of the lock-out, while the employers made much of the argument that the American machinists' extra hours gave their industry a competitive advantage, Barnes's reply was to say that this situation could not last:

America is living on its vitals, and labour is being used up at a rate which must inevitably lead to its organization.[3]

The ideas of Frederick W. Taylor, the pioneer of scientific management, were already beginning to influence shop practice, and the systematic "speed-up" of work was a matter of complaint among American industrial workers. But the gravity of the situa-

[1] Perlman and Taft, *op. cit.*, iv, 169.
[2] This view is well stated in *Amalgamated Engineers Journal*, Jan. 1901, pp. 2 f.
[3] *Amalgamated Engineers Journal*, May 1899, p. 5.

tion was exaggerated in Britain. One returned immigrant, writing in the *Newcastle Daily Leader*, said:

The workmen apparently worked harder than they do here. There was plenty of young blood, but very little of the old in the workshops, and I could not help reflecting upon the pathos which its absence suggested. "Where are your older men?" I asked. The reply came, "Oh, there are very few old men here; they either die off or go up the country." Old age is sacrificed for young blood. It is a progressing policy, and will . . . inspire a terrible reaction in the near future of American industrialism.[1]

It is possible that the visiting Englishman was deceived by the high proportion of younger people that he saw in America, owing to the heavy rate of immigration, into believing that the old had died off earlier. Statistics were sometimes produced to show that Americans had a lower expectation of life than people in Britain, but it could never be argued with any degree of certainty that this was due to the strain of American industrial life.[2]

These various trade unionist interpretations of the American scene were put to the test in 1902 by a unique experiment carried out by Alfred Mosely, a wealthy South African mine-owner. Mosely, impressed by the efficiency of American labour and management, decided to send two commissions to America, one, consisting of trade union leaders, to study industrial conditions, and the other, composed of experts in various fields of education, to examine all phases of the American educational system. The trade union team consisted of twenty-three members, representing all principal manufacturing and building trades. In order to leave the delegates free to come to their own conclusions, Mosely allowed them to concentrate on their own trades, and to present individual reports as well as to answer a general questionnaire.[3]

---

[1] *Newcastle Daily Leader*, 2 Jan. 1902, quoted *Amalgamated Engineers Journal*, Feb. 1902, pp. 14 f.

[2] See E. Levasseur, *The American Workman* (Baltimore, 1900), pp. 82–5, for the fast pace of working life. A. Maurice Low noted that the English worker was "inclined to believe that the American working man is earlier 'scrapped' than the British working man" (*Bulletin of the Bureau of Labor*, No. 50 (Jan. 1904), p. 3). But the view was not confined to the worker: Steevens (*Land of the Dollar*, pp. 314 f.) thought that the climate and the "strenuous fever of life" were responsible for early death.

[3] Mosely Industrial Commission, *Reports of the Delegates* (London, 1903), (quoted hereafter as *M.I.C.R.*), preface by Alfred Mosely. See also an interview

Moseley had the idea that the tour would open the eyes of the trade union leaders to the uselessness of old restrictive practices; but he over-estimated the degree to which such practices were really believed in or encouraged by responsible union leaders such as those whom he sent to America. On this score, the commissioners had nothing to disavow.[1] What was new to them was the fact that in most of the areas they visited in the industrial North, the American workers were not merely better off than the British, in spite of a higher cost of living, but were not more hard-worked. Barnes, who had already committed himself most fully to the theory of overwork in America, clung to some statistics to show that "prolonged daily strain" was a factor in limiting the average life of the American machinist;[2] but few of his colleagues could find much substance for the charge. "In Mr. Carnegie's works at Homestead, if anywhere," said W. C. Steadman,

I expected to see them stripped to the waist; but nothing of the kind. While turning out a lot of work they took things very gently.[3]

Even James Macdonald, a member of the Social-Democratic Federation, was obliged to admit:

Of the hustling and bustling which we had been led to believe greets you on every hand, I met none of it, at least not in the factories or workshops.[4]

The visitors, including Macdonald, were strongly impressed by the friendly relationship of management and labour, and

with Mosely in the *Daily Mail*, 1 Feb. 1902; and an interview with James Macdonald in *Justice*, 10 Jan. 1903.

[1] The case of W. Abraham, Liberal M.P. and President of the South Wales Miners' Federation, must have been unique. Returning from a visit to America in 1902, he admitted that "he returned thoroughly cured of the prejudice [against the use of machinery] and would in future advocate . . . the use of machinery to produce things necessary to maintain Great Britain in competition with other countries." *The Times*, 9 Apr. 1902. But Abraham was not on the Mosely Commission, which included no miners.

[2] *M.I.C.R.*, p. 76. Shortly before his visit to America, Barnes was expressing the fear that American sub-division of labour was breeding "a type of workman far inferior to the mechanics of this country in initiative" and far below the Ruskinian ideal of "happy-hearted human creatures" (*Review of Reviews*, 15 Aug. 1901, supplement p. 6). Keir Hardie drew his impressions of American industry from Barnes—see *Labour Leader*, 6 Dec. 1902.

[3] *M.I.C.R.*, pp. 257 f.

[4] *London Trades and Labour Gazette*, Jan. 1903.

noticed how much more accessible the managers were to their workers.[1]

The principal conclusions of the delegates about the advantages of American industry have a strangely modern ring. First of all, the American educational system was superior to that of Britain, and provided much better training for all types of industrial occupations. This point was later confirmed by the Mosely Educational Commission.[2] Secondly, in the words of Alexander Wilkie, secretary of the Shipwrights:

The three outstanding features of American industry appear to me to be its tendency towards greater centralization . . . the specialization of industry and the subdivision of labour . . . and labour-saving machinery.[3]

This, after all, was only what the spokesmen of trade unionism had emphasized in the past as the cause of American competitive success. They had no objection to it, provided that it was linked with a system of high wages. One of the most interesting reports, in this connection, was that of C. W. Bowerman, of the London Society of Compositors, who visited the plant of the National Cash Register Works at Dayton, Ohio, and was startled by a large notice which read "Improved Machinery Makes Men Dearer, Their Products Cheaper."[4] In the Chicago printing

[1] It is probable that the visitors saw only the more efficient plants: but most trade union leaders were sufficiently alert to make allowances for that.

[2] *Reports of the Mosely Educational Commission* (Manchester, 1904). See esp. p. xxiii of the Joint Report: "Although, in the past, the belief in education has been the effect rather than the cause of American prosperity, during the last quarter of a century education has had a powerful and far-reaching influence and it cannot be doubted that, in the future, it will become more and more the cause of industrial and commercial progress and of national well-being." Mosely's own views were even more definite: "It is my firm belief that the public school system of the United States is the most potent factor in the commercial supremacy of this nation" (*The Times*, 14 Dec. 1903). In 1906–7 he arranged for several hundred school teachers to visit the United States and Canada.

[3] *M.I.C.R.*, p. 96. The same conclusion was arrived at by John Hodge, secretary of the Steel-smelters, who in 1901 had persuaded his union to send him to visit American tinplate works so that he could challenge the statements about them by employers at the meetings of the Tinplate Board. See Hodge, *Workman's Cottage to Windsor Castle* (London, 1931), pp. 290–6.

[4] *M.I.C.R.*, p. 225.

establishments Bowerman marvelled at the anxiety of the employers to keep up with the most up-to-date improvements by constantly replacing their machinery. His colleague, G. D. Kelley of the Lithographic Printers, agreed: "The number of labour-saving appliances in use for almost everything is perfectly astounding."[1]

Nearly all the delegates preferred to speak of their own trades rather that to generalize about all American industry: which was sensible enough, as they were only in the United States for about a month. However, W. C. Steadman, who attended as the representative of the Parliamentary Committee of the T.U.C., considered it his duty to draw some general conclusions:

The English worker has nothing to learn from America, but the employers have a lot. Let our employers realize that labour is as much a partner in the business as his capital, and that the success or failure of that business depends upon both. . . . High wages pay both the employer and the employed. In America they know this, and act up to it; hence the secret of their success. The trade unions in this country have been accused of driving the trade out of the country, yet the same forces at work here are working there, only more so, for trade unionism in that country is increasing by leaps and bounds as a purely industrial and fighting force, and yet America is going ahead.[2]

Mosely had hoped that the delegation's visit would lead its members to take a strong stand against "ca'canny" and other restrictive devices on their return to Britain, and he persuaded them all to recommend the introduction to Britain of a "National Civic Federation" of the American type, for the voluntary discussion and, if possible, solution of matters affecting capital and labour, by representatives of the two sides.[3] But nothing came of

---

[1] M.I.C.R., p. 237. For a very interesting discussion of the position in the printing trades at this time, see G. Binney Dibblee, "The Printing Trades and the Crisis in British Industry," *Economic Journal*, xii (1902), 1–14. Dibblee, a Fellow of All Souls and Manager of the *Manchester Guardian*, diagnosed the trouble as follows: "We have not the same level of ability to draw upon for our employing class as the newer country. . . . The best of the brains of our upper classes will go anywhere but into industry."

[2] M.I.C.R., pp. 259 f.

[3] *Ibid.*, p. 11. The National Civic Federation was a development of the Civic Federation founded in Chicago in 1893, largely on the initiative of W. T. Stead. In 1902 Senator Mark Hanna was its chairman and Samuel Gompers its vice-chairman. For the attempt to form a Civic Federation in

the Civic Federation idea, partly because some machinery of
conciliation already existed, partly also because many employers
and trade unionists were in no mood for further conciliation after
Taff Vale.[1]

What, then, had the members of the commission learnt from
their travels? They had found that the occasional violence of
American strikes did not preclude much easier and more informal
relations between management and men than in British industry.
And this informality, they realized, was an indication of the
much higher status of the manual worker in American society.
He was better educated, both for work and for community life;
and the recognition of his value had been a powerful factor
in stimulating invention and the introduction of labour-saving
devices.

The general conclusion, therefore, was that the progress of
American industry, in so far as it was not due to purely geographical advantages, was due much more to labour-saving devices than
to any other factor. Longer hours and the absence of unionism
were neither of them factors of any significance.[2] As Steadman
pointed out, the American trade union movement was able
to make sensational advances just at the time when the delegation
was in America. All these facts, damaging though they were to
any such dogmatic generalization as that of the Marxist thesis of
increasing misery, could yet form a justification of the main

London, see *Daily News*, 15 Jan. and 5 Mar. 1903. A body called the National
Industrial Association, to which some of the less radical union leaders belonged,
was altered to follow the American pattern more closely. But it never made
any headway. For its initiation, see Mantoux and Alfassa, *La Crise du Trade-
Unionisme*, pp. 225–34.

[1] It is noteworthy that the support for Compulsory Arbitration at the
T.U.C. dropped from 35 per cent of the vote in 1901 to 24 per cent in 1902
and 22 per cent in 1903; it increased again later.

[2] Ben Tillett (secretary of the London Dockers) and F. Chandler (secretary
of the Amalgamated Society of Carpenters and Joiners) came to a similar
conclusion as a result of their visit as fraternal delegates to the A.F.L. Convention in Dec. 1901. They contradicted not only the view "that American industrial prosperity is due to the absence of trade unionism" but also the idea of
"excessive toil and servile workmen working for low wages in America."—
T.U.C. *Report*, 1902, pp. 52–4. Tillett marvelled at the fact that Senator Mark
Hanna, the great industrialist, was to be seen in an expensive hotel in the
company of "happy little bands of artisans and their families."—Ben Tillett,
Memories and Reflections (London, 1931), p. 226.

defensive arguments of the leaders of British trade unionism against *The Times* attacks.

Ironically, indeed, the outcome of the Mosely Commission was that *The Times* was compelled to admit error in assessing the industrial situation in America. A leading article blandly made the admission in such a way as to leave the unions in both countries under the cloud of authoritative disapproval:

The highly interesting letters in which our correspondent with Mr. Mosely's Commission in America has described the impressions produced upon him by the trip appear to show that the conditions of labour in the two countries present fewer points of difference than has commonly been supposed. The American employer is by no means exempt from the hindrances to business occasioned by strikers among his workers, nor are the strikes always of such a character as to command or to deserve sympathy. . . . On a review of all the circumstances, our Correspondent is plainly justified in his opinion that the American employer has no reason to be specially grateful to the labour organizations.[1]

It was a pity, however, that *The Times* failed to pursue the enquiry into industrial efficiency along the lines suggested by the Commission: for there is little doubt that in these years at the beginning of the present century British industry needed the spur of a public demand for increased productivity. A few of the political leaders of the time, notably the Liberal League under Rosebery, realized the need for what Sidney Webb called "A Policy of National Efficiency."[2] Unfortunately, the discussion was diverted from the main path into the controversial tangles of fiscal policy, after Joseph Chamberlain made his tariff proposals in 1903. This, combined with the superficial prosperity of the later Edwardian years and the revival of overseas investment, put the more important issues into the background until after the First World War.

*   *   *

It now becomes possible to redraw the picture of trade union

[1] *The Times*, 27 Dec. 1902.
[2] S. Webb, *A Policy of National Efficiency* (Fabian Tract No. 108, Nov. 1901); *Liberal League Manifesto* (London, May 1902); and Liberal League publications, notably No. 33 (Lord Rosebery, *Administrative Efficiency*, 1902) and No. 64 (*Wanted! Efficiency, not Tariffs*, 1903).

G

attitudes to the formation of a Labour Party at the turn of the century. The course of events in America, as interpreted by the British labour movement, seemed to give much weight to the argument in favour of independent parliamentary representation. Ramsay MacDonald, the secretary of the Labour Representation Committee, emphasized in his first official circular the growing power of "federated capital," and its strength in Parliament.[1] The news from America seemed to show that "federated capital" and, still more, concentrated capital could cause great damage to labour, especially if it could strongly influence or control the political machine. It is true that in the event there was no development of trusts in Britain on any scale comparable with that in America. The expectation nevertheless existed; and Socialist propaganda, especially that of the Marxists, fastened on the American example as an indication of what was in store for Britain. "Nearly all of us revolutionary Social-Democrats," said Hyndman, "are drawing our clearest illustration of the approaching and inevitable transformation of capitalism from America."[2]

Not all the trade union leaders were readily disposed to accept as gospel everything that the Socialists said: but they were converted by the employers, whose unbounded enthusiasm for supposed American conditions of employer-labour relationship aroused the suspicions of Socialist and non-Socialist alike. Consequently, even before the conclusion of the main Taff Vale Case, there was a tendency of the whole trade union movement to close its ranks in support of a demand for a separate Labour Party. This was clearly indicated by Pete Curran, the chairman of the General Federation of Trade Unions, in a statement written just before the Taff Vale decision of 1901:

[1] Labour Representation Committee *First Circular*, 23 Mar. 1900.
[2] Hyndman to H. G. Wilshire, 13 Feb. 1901, quoted in *Challenge* (Los Angeles), 13 Mar. 1901. Less optimistic than Hyndman, though not less influenced by the American example, was the Socialist novelist H. G. Wells, who in his *When the Sleeper Wakes* (London, 1899) envisaged a period of two centuries in which the trust would develop its power over the people. Wells wrote (p. 171): "Power was passing even in Victorian times to the party machinery, secret, complex, and corrupt. Very speedily power was in the hand of great men of business who financed the machines. . . . In most of these things America was a little earlier than England, though both countries drove the same way."

There is at present a general outcry in this country from a large section of the property owners that if we do not resort to more rapid methods of producing wealth we will be entirely beaten out of the field even in our own markets. I find that this general craze among sections of the people is wedding closer the bonds of sympathy and united effort between the extreme and the more moderate wings of the trade union movement, as this craze threatens the possibility of that systematic method of driving which is so common in America.[1]

For the time being, at least, the ears of the non-Socialists were open to the propaganda of the Socialists, especially those who had paid some attention to the trust problem. Thus the Fabian economist, H. W. Macrosty, was given space in the annual report of the General Federation of Trade Unions, published in June 1901, to discuss the effect of trusts on the working class. Macrosty's conclusion was that they would damage the workers' position, unless political action was taken: "If the workers will not rule the country, the trusts will."[2]

The Taff Vale case and *The Times* attacks were deciding factors in bringing the trade unions to the support of the Labour Representation Committee. "The *Thunderer* has done us a good turn," said D. C. Cummings of the Boilermakers;[3] and so it had, without any intention of so doing. As the Committee's 1902 report put it:

Menaced on every hand in workshop, court of law, and press, Trade Unionism has no refuge except the ballot box and Labour Representation.[4]

The Amalgamated Society of Engineers, for instance, voted by five to one to join, thus reversing an earlier decision to abstain; the new vote was taken in January 1902, in the midst of the principal *Times* attack and just six months after the Taff Vale

[1] Letter dated 19 July 1901, printed in *International Socialist Review* (Chicago) Sept. 1901, pp. 185–7. The Taff Vale case was decided by the Lords on 22 July; *Quinn* v. *Leatham* on 5 Aug. Curran had visited America in 1900–1 as T.U.C. fraternal delegate to the A.F.L. convention. See "Interview with Pete Curran," *Labour Leader*, 2 Feb. 1901.

[2] H. W. Macrosty, "Trusts and the Workman," G.F.T.U. *Annual Report*, 1901, p. 25.

[3] *London Trades and Labour Gazette*, May 1902.

[4] L.R.C. *Report*, 1902, p. 12.

decision.[1] Even more notable was the adhesion of the Textile
Workers, well known for their caution in political matters. In
May 1902 the *Cotton Factory Times*, which was a labour paper,
had advised its readers to study the problems of the trusts and to
"prepare their plans to counteract the evils that will arise."[2] The
main element in the union leaders' plans was labour representation.
Consequently, the total affiliated membership of the L.R.C. rose
rapidly from 375,931 in 1901 to 851,150 two years later;[3] and at
the 1903 conference it was decided to set up a Parliamentary Fund
to pay the election expenses of Labour candidates and their
maintenance if elected. Although this increased the subscription
rate to the party by more than nine times, the membership, after
a very slight drop in 1904–5, thereafter continued to grow.

In half a dozen years at the turn of the century, the alliance of
Labour and Socialism had been forged which was to bring their
joint political party in due course to office and to power. In that
process the image of America, as seen by trade union leaders and
radicals in Britain, had played a significant role. It was widely
assumed that the existing state of America reflected the future
state of Britain; and that the existing state of America was an
unhappy one for the worker. Although both these assumptions
were at least partially mistaken, they did their work. The Mosely
Commission removed some of the trade union leaders' misap-
prehensions, but did nothing to break down the alignment of
capital against labour in Britain. The Labour Party was born, and
on its very birthday its denunciation of "the American experience"
was at least as sharp and as bitter as its criticism of the state of
things inside Britain.

---

1 *Amalgamated Engineers Journal*, Feb. 1902, p. 65.
2 *Cotton Factory Times*, 2 May 1902. I owe this reference to Mr. Frank
Bealey.
3 L.R.C. *Report*, 1903, p. 11.

CHAPTER VI

AMERICA AND THE BRITISH "LABOUR UNREST"

IN studying the successful foundation of the British Labour Party on Socialist initiative, we must not forget the fact that in America, too, Socialism achieved prominence as a political force. The Socialist Party of America was founded in 1901 by a fusion of Debs's Social Democratic Party and a large breakaway from De Leon's Socialist Labor Party. The latter, best known as the S.L.P., continued to exist without much growth as a sectional group in the New York area, its membership consisting largely of immigrants. The Socialist Party, on the other hand, made rapid progress in developing a nation-wide organization. In 1912 its Presidential ticket polled altogether 900,000 votes, in spite of the competition of an independent Progressive candidate, Theodore Roosevelt. The party's total membership in the same year reached a peak of 135,000, which was almost exactly six times as large as the largest Socialist party in Britain, the I.L.P., at that time.[1]

The American Socialists, however, lacked the political influence of the British I.L.P., because they had no comparable tie with the organized labour movement. The reasons for the failure of the American Federation of Labor, under Samuel Gompers, to join the Socialists in a political alliance have frequently been subjected to analysis, and a number of factors can readily be enumerated. The absence of a tradition of class consciousness in America delayed the growth of the unions, and made them reluctant to associate their own industrial struggles with those of all other manual workers. This reluctance was strengthened as increasing

---

[1] David A. Shannon, *Socialist Party of America* (New York, 1955), p. 78. I.L.P. affiliation fees for 1912–13 suggest an average membership of under 23,000: see *I.L.P. Conference Report*, 1913, p. 35.

numbers of heterogeneous immigrants used to low standards of living entered the country at the end of the nineteenth century. Compared with the British unions, the A.F.L. was smaller in proportion to the total labour force, more exclusive, and more narrowly craft-conscious. Socialistic aims, which in both countries appealed most strongly to the less skilled, had little to offer Gompers and his colleagues.

Under these circumstances the American Socialist movement failed to secure any institutional link with organized labour, and consequently, being dependent to a large extent on the support of "intellectuals," tended to become more extreme and violent in language than the British movement as a whole.[1] Certainly in Britain, as we shall see, Socialist extremists were to be found: but the centre of gravity of the movement was much further to the right. Thus John Spargo, who had belonged to the S.D.F. in Britain and was consequently regarded as one of the intransigents, after emigrating to America took his place among the moderates of the Socialist Party without any noticeable change in his views. It is probable that in 1909 a majority of the committee of the Socialist Party of America was in favour of an alliance with the unions: but nothing came of it, and the majority view was kept secret, as one of the leaders said, for fear of a "public scandal."[2] This was the year in which the adhesion of the Miners' Federation made the labour alliance in Britain virtually complete, so far as the major unions were concerned.

*   *   *

The British Socialists were puzzled by the differences between their own movement and that in America. It was still their view that the growth of trusts in American industry, and the bitterness of labour-employer relations there, would lead to an earlier

---

[1] H. G. Wells described it as "reeking with class feeling and class hatred . . . far more closely akin to the revolutionary Socialism of the continent of Europe than to the constructive and evolutionary Socialism of Great Britain." Wells, *Social Forces in England and America* (New York, 1914), pp. 345 f. This was a harsh judgment, especially on the former Populists of the Middle West, with whom Wells probably had not come in contact.

[2] Ira Kipnis, *American Socialist Movement, 1897–1912* (New York, 1952), p. 229.

dénouement of the class struggle than in Europe. The more Marxist of them believed in the inevitability of this process: the less dogmatic, like Keir Hardie, were inclined to place stress on the need for a consolidation of the working-class movement under a wise leadership, which would bring the unions and the Socialists together. On his return from a transatlantic tour in 1909, Hardie wrote:

Capitalism has a power of adaptability for which some of its Socialist opponents do not make sufficient allowance. The one thing that will bring Socialism soon is a big, genuine working-class movement around which the better element of American citizenship could rally.[1]

For Hardie and the other I.L.P. leaders, it seemed necessary that the American Socialists should follow the same course as they themselves had taken in Britain, and should create a Labour Party after successfully permeating the unions. The British leaders hardly stopped to weigh the special difficulties of this course in the existing state of American society. At times, they affected a smug complacency about their own superior wisdom in effecting an alliance with the unions. Thus Ramsay MacDonald, now a Member of Parliament, could describe the A.F.L. leaders as "men whose political genius is of a low order";[2] and J. R. Clynes, also a Labour M.P., could write, on returning from a visit to America, that

American trade unions, in point of political activities, stand now where ours did fifteen years ago. American industrial legislation compared with ours is twenty years behind, and the American Socialist bodies suggest no comparison with ours at any time.[3]

To the I.L.P. leaders, the closest approximation to their own tactics were those employed by the Milwaukee Socialists led by Victor Berger, who with the support of the local trades council were able to control the city administration for two years, and put into effect a policy of municipal Socialism on Fabian lines.[4] When Berger was elected to Congress, MacDonald commented:

[1] *Socialist Review*, iii (1909), p. 94.   [2] *Ibid.*, ii (1908), p. 565.
[3] *Labour Leader*, 24 Dec. 1909. Cf. the view of Robert Smillie (*My Life for Labour* (London, 1924), p. 149), based on a visit of 1912, that America was "fifteen or twenty years behind."
[4] For a brief account, see Henry Pelling, "Rise and Decline of Socialism in Milwaukee," *Bulletin of the Int. Inst. Soc. Hist.*, 1955, pp. 91–103.

Through good and ill report he has stood for such a policy as we ourselves are fighting [for]. . . . No one is more worthy to be the first in America to win the laurels of victory.[1]

The members of the S.D.F., on the other hand, were satisfied to regard themselves as the British counterpart of the Socialist Party of America. Considering the British Labour Party to be a failure, they were pleased to see that no such alliance with the unions had been effected in the United States. To the annoyance of the I.L.P. leaders, Hyndman and his associates worked hard and not without some success to persuade the American Socialists that the S.D.F. was the really representative Socialist organization of Britain.[2]

At the same time, both I.L.P. and S.D.F. members were agreed on the main characteristics of the American scene. For all of them, America was the country where capitalism was most brutal and where class lines were becoming most sharply defined. This was partly the result of items of news that came across the Atlantic, many of which led them to an immediately unfavourable contrast with what was customary in British conditions. For instance, they were shocked by the severity of American courts in granting injunctions against the unions, as in the Danbury Hatters and the Bucks' Stove cases;[3] and they were amazed by the violence which took place in the course of various labour conflicts, especially those involving the Western Federation of Miners and the I.W.W.[4] Meanwhile, the American Socialists themselves—many of them much more extreme than their British comrades—continued to emphasize the more startling elements in the American scene. This was the heyday of the literature of protest in America—a literature which interpreted in terms of class conflict the "unsophisticated violence of American life that appealed to Europeans."[5] The British Socialist could, and often did, take his idea of high finance from Frank Norris, his analysis of class conflict

[1] *Socialist Review*, vi (1910), p. 241.

[2] *International Socialist Review* (Chicago), *passim*. For I.L.P. annoyance, see *Socialist Review*, vi (1910), p. 87.

[3] For comment, see *Labour Leader*, 24 July and 2 Oct. 1908; *Social-Democrat*, xii (1908), 76 f.

[4] See, e.g., the accounts of Bill Haywood's tour of the branches of the S.D.P. (formerly S.D.F.) in 1910, *Justice*, 15 and 29 Oct. 1910.

[5] R. E. Spiller, *et. al.*, *Literary History of the United States* (New York, 1948), ii, 1375.

from Jack London and his description of the lot of the immigrant from Upton Sinclair.[1] A *Justice* reviewer described London's *Iron Heel*, with its vivid picture of a ruthless civil war, as a "nightmare" and a "warning" for the workers:[2] that its standpoint was widely accepted is clear from the constant repetition in the British Socialist press of remarks such as "There is no better organized or more brutal class than the capitalists of America" (Hyndman);[3] that, whatever the present state of its labour movement, America was somehow "ahead of us" because of "sheer desperation for immediate Government regulation of big industries" (R. J. Campbell);[4] and that consequently the future held for the American Socialists a "splendid opportunity" (Clynes),[5] so that, because "America always moves quickly" (Keir Hardie)[6], one could conclude that "Truly, the day is not far distant when the Red Flag will wave over the Capitol at Washington" (Tom Quelch).[7]

One section of the British Socialists could not share this optimism. This was the Fabian element. Always inclined to emphasize the importance of state control and bureaucratic efficiency, the Fabians could not but be aghast at the complex of constitutional deadlock and administrative corruption that the United States presented. Sidney Webb, while touring America in 1898, wrote to Bernard Shaw to say that "this people, in all that concerns the *machinery* of government, is infantile."[8] In 1906 H. G. Wells, then in his Fabian phase, reported the absence of "that living sense of the state out of which constructive effort must arise,"[9] and in the following year Bernard Shaw, who did not bother to conduct investigations on the spot, spoke of the American scene as a "tragi-comedy of the Virtuous Villager and the Bold Bad Trust": the Americans, he said, could not nationalize

[1] The principal works here referred to are: Frank Norris, *The Octopus* (1901) and *The Pit* (1903); Jack London, *The War of the Classes* (1905) and *The Iron Heel* (1907); and Upton Sinclair, *The Jungle* (1906) and *The Metropolis* (1908).

[2] *Justice*, 20 Feb. 1909.   [3] *Ibid.*, 8 Oct. 1910.
[4] *Labour Leader*, 23 Dec. 1912.   [5] *Ibid.*, 24 Dec. 1909.
[6] *Socialist Review*, x (1912), 265.   [7] *Justice*, 4 May 1912.
[8] Webb to Shaw, 26 Apr. 1898, Webb Papers, Brit. Lib. Pol. Sci.
[9] H. G. Wells, *The Future in America* (London, 1906), p. 233.

the trusts for lack of "not only a powerful government but highly capable administrative departments of permanent civil servants."[1] Having said all this, the Fabian leaders felt able to forget about America; and it was only a small minority of left-wing intellectuals who continued to interest themselves in aspects of American government, and to take the trouble to examine such developments as the "Wisconsin Idea."[2] In their world tour of 1911–12, which took them through Canada to Japan and India, the Webbs did not pause to examine the progress of the Republic.

In one respect, however, there was an important coincidence of view between the Fabians and almost all sections of the British left. This was in their attitude to Scientific Management—an indisputably American invention. The early pioneers of Scientific Management had done little to soothe the natural suspicions of organized labour about the system, and in 1911 the Executive Council of the American Federation of Labor condemned it as "calculated to drive workmen beyond the point necessary to their safety, increasing accidents, and undermining their health."[3] At this time British employers in the engineering and shipbuilding industries had begun to introduce the Premium Bonus system, and although the Amalgamated Society of Engineers, the biggest union in the industries, accepted it in an agreement of 1902, its working led to an enquiry and an emphatic condemnation of it by the T.U.C. at its 1910 Congress.[4] The more general aspects of Scientific Management had however attracted little attention in Britain, and although Frederick W. Taylor, the most notable of the protagonists of the system in America, was anxious to see it

[1] G. Bernard Shaw, "A Nation of Villagers," *Everybody's Magazine*, xvii (New York, 1907), pp. 861–4.

[2] For Alfred Zimmern's pilgrimage to Madison, Wisconsin, to see the co-operation of university professors and state administrators in the time of the elder LaFollette, see his letter to Graham Wallas, 24 Dec. 1911, Wallas Papers. J. A. Hobson also visited Madison but seems to have been depressed by the naïvety of William Jennings Bryan, whom he met there, J. A. Hobson, *Confessions of an Economic Heretic* (London, 1938), pp. 69 f.

[3] *American Federationist*, xvii (1911), p. 110.

[4] J. B. Jefferys, *Story of the Engineers* (London, 1945), p. 155; T.U.C. *Annual Report*, 1909, pp. 74, 186, and 1910, p. 71. See also *Amalgamated Engineers Journal*, Aug. 1911, pp. 21–7; J. T. Brownlie, "Evils of the Premium Bonus System," *Social-Democrat*, xv (1911), p. 200.

spread to Britain, and enlisted the keen interest of the British Ambassador in the United States, James Bryce, he was unable to secure much response from British employers.[1] One ironmaster in Yorkshire, to whom Taylor sent a copy of his *Principles of Scientific Management*, startled him by reciprocating with a work of his own—an edition of Horace's *Odes* in the original.[2] News of the application of the system in America, and copies of Taylor's book or other works such as Hugo Munsterburg's *Psychology and Industrial Efficiency* (1913) apprised the educated British public of the importance of the subject, and several discussions took place in the left-wing journals which indicated considerable nervousness about the impact of the American methods on British labour, and a feeling that they ignored the human element in industry. Margaret Bondfield, a leading women's trade unionist and I.L.P. member, who had spent five months in America in 1910, wrote to the London *Nation*, quoting the McKee's Rock strike of 1909 to show "the dangers inherent in the American methods";[3] and Beatrice Webb, reviewing Munsterburg's book in the new Fabian weekly the *New Statesman*, declared that

The whole of this movement in the United States, from its inception in the Harvard psychological laboratories to its application by the great capitalist trusts, seems a shocking instance of short-sighted materialism.[4]

Beatrice Webb had also been highly critical of Taylor's book, and regarded American syndicalism as largely a reaction to rash experiments in Scientific Management. After reading the

[1] Bryce to Taylor, 23 Jan. 1913, F. W. Taylor Papers, Stevens Institute of Technology, Hoboken, N.J. See also Frank B. Copley, *Frederick W. Taylor* (New York, 1923), ii, 410 f. Bryce was no friend of labour and had abandoned the easy optimism of the *Essays on Reform* by now. He wrote to his old friend Dicey on 13 Dec. 1911 deploring the "upcoming of labour into politics" which had "lowered the spirit and tone of public life" and "fundamentally changed . . . the whole problem of democratic government as we regarded it when we wrote those essays in 1866-7." (Bryce Papers.)

[2] J. H. Wicksteed to Taylor, 4 Mar. 1913, Taylor Papers.

[3] *Nation*, 17 Aug. 1912. For an account of the strike at McKee's Rock, Pennsylvania, see Perlman and Taft, *History of Labor in the U.S.*, iv, 263-5.

[4] *New Statesman*, 26 Apr. 1913. The article was unsigned, and I am grateful to Mr. Kingsley Martin, the present editor of the *New Statesman and Nation*, for confirming Mrs. Webb's authorship from his files.

Principles of Scientific Management, she wrote to her friend Lady Betty Balfour:

Do not go and send this book to English Labour and Socialist friends. It is the only justification I have yet read for the policy of Sabotage.[1]

Mrs. Webb's attitude is especially interesting in view of her husband's early enthusiasm for the Premium Bonus system, which he had described in 1902 as "an admirable expedient."[2]

What was needed, of course, was some evidence of applications of the system in Britain. In 1914 a discussion of the subject by various industrial experts and economists, reprinted in the *Sociological Review*, revealed that Taylor's principles had been successfully put into operation in at least one place—the engineering works of Hans Renold Ltd. at Manchester.[3] J. A. Hobson, in the same discussion, gave a warning that

Under Scientific Management there is no guarantee that only those economies which involve no increase of human costs shall be adopted.[4]

G. D. H. Cole, a young Oxford don who was winning prominence as a Socialist writer on labour problems, went further and maintained positively that the system would "make the worker's lot more monotonous" and also "be fatal to effective trade unionism."[5] Finally, when G. C. Allingham, one of Taylor's few apostles in Britain,[6] lectured on the subject to the Junior Institute of Engineers, Richard Whiteing, the Radical novelist, commented in the Socialist weekly the *Clarion* under the heading "Speeding Them Up: Another Step towards Industrial Slavery":

Even in Republican America, where the worker has been brought to heel more effectually than in any other part of the planet, this new development of the Boss system is a feature of the Taylor scheme that has met with the greatest opposition. . . . There seems no reason why the man should not finally become indistinguishable from the machine,

---

[1] Beatrice Webb to Lady Betty Balfour, 16 Oct. 1912, Webb Papers.
[2] *Amalgamated Engineers Journal*, Oct. 1902.
[3] C. G. Renold (b. 1883), the son of Hans Renold, had been educated at Cornell University. See his *Joint Consultation over Thirty Years* (London, 1950).
[4] *Sociological Review*, vii (1914), p. 118.   [5] *Ibid.*, p. 120.
[6] Allingham's brother Henry worked for Hans Renold Ltd.

and so develop into a new type of the race. America has a long and notable record in the attempt to invent a perfect fusion of them.[1]

Whatever the situation in America, it would be naïve to suppose that "Taylorism" was a *direct* cause of industrial unrest in Britain at this time.[2] As we have seen, British industry hardly felt the impact of the new methods, and even the Premium Bonus system can hardly have affected the industries which were most concerned in the "labour unrest"—mining and transport. W. H. Quinn of the Bookbinders was unnecessarily alarmist when at the Labour Party Conference in 1912 he spoke of "a tendency in the direction of Americanizing British industry . . . a speeding-up of machinery and a speeding-up of men," which he declared had caused "a greater amount of unrest in the workshop at the present time than there had been in the history of British industry."[3] The unrest was due in large part to a much more general phenomenon —the rising cost of living, which, by contrast with the years before 1900, demanded a more militant policy on the part of the unions if the workers were so much as to hold their own with a steady real wage level. Another important factor was the prevailing dissatisfaction with the Parliamentary Labour Party, which seemed to have drifted into alliance with the Liberals and to be unable to fulfil the high hopes of 1906.

Nevertheless, as the ensuing discussion will seek to show, the views held in Britain about American political and industrial conditions did play a part in the unrest of the time. If the British workers could not yet experience the American conditions which they feared, they certainly had their fears: *omne ignotum pro magnifico* may be the conclusion of the social historian on the contemporary British labour view of America.

★   ★   ★

There were numerous "movements" in the early twentieth century which may be said to have made distinctive contributions to the "labour unrest" of the years before the First World War.

---

[1] *Clarion*, 20 Dec. 1913.
[2] For a fuller—but still incomplete—discussion of the topic, see L. Urwick and E. F. L. Brech, *Making of Scientific Management*, ii (London, 1949), ch. vii.
[3] Labour Party, *Annual Report*, 1912, p. 87.

The first to make its appearance was the Socialist Labour Party, which was formed in 1903 by a secession of members of the S.D.F., mostly in Scotland, who had come under the influence of De Leon's Socialist Labor Party in America. This group had been of importance in persuading the S.D.F. leaders to withdraw from the Labour Representation Committee, which they did in 1901, just over a year after it had been founded. But the group remained dissatisfied with the S.D.F. leadership, and in particular with the domineering veteran, H. M. Hyndman. In 1902 the dissentients, among whom the Irishman James Connolly was prominent, began to use De Leon's *Weekly People*, of New York, to express their defiance of Hyndman and his associates. Soon, they were able to found a paper of their own, the Edinburgh *Socialist*, which advertised the literature of the American S.L.P. and especially the works of De Leon. Both in Scotland and in London evening classes were established for the study of Marxism, the texts used being normally the translations published by the American Socialist presses.[1]

About the time of the establishment of the S.L.P. in Britain, De Leon himself began to take up industrial unionism—that is to say, the idea that each industry should have only one union catering for all its workers irrespective of their status or skill. In American industry there was a strong case for such a development, for two reasons: first, because of the rapid growth of large factories where jobs were minutely specialized; and secondly, because, as we have seen, the unions in America so far catered only for a small 'aristocratic' fraction of the aggregate of workers. Neither of these reasons could be said to apply with similar force in Britain: but naturally for the newly-born S.L.P. of Britain the arguments of De Leon had particular weight. In January 1904 the *Socialist* published a leader on "The Americanization of British Trade Unionism," which argued that the existing unions were

---

[1] T. A. Jackson, *Solo Trumpet* (London, 1903), p. 61, tells of reading *Value, Price and Profit* and *Eighteenth Brumaire of Louis Napoleon* this way. Jackson also subscribed to the *Weekly People*. See also Tom Bell, *Pioneering Days* (London, 1941), pp. 37 f.; J. T. Murphy in Arthur Gleason, *What the Workers Want* (New York, 1920), p. 203. The best account of the origin of the S.L.P. is C. Tsuzuki, "The Impossibilist Revolt in Britain," to be published in the *International Review of Social History* in 1956.

becoming corrupt and undemocratic. In the course of the same year, De Leon himself visited Britain on his way home from the International Socialist Congress at Amsterdam. In 1905, therefore, the British party was ready to follow at once the American S.L.P.'s initiative in propounding the gospel of Industrial Unionism, and to acclaim the newly-founded Industrial Workers of the World (I.W.W.), which was inaugurated with the co-operation of De Leon at a conference in Chicago in June. Members of the British S.L.P. at once founded a body called the "Advocates of Industrial Unionism," which later changed its name to the "Industrial Workers of Great Britain."

It was perhaps a natural development that one of the strongest branches of the Advocates of Industrial Unionism should be in the Singer Sewing Machine works at Kilbowie, Clydebank, which employed some 12,000 workers. Singers was primarily an American firm, but it had established itself in Europe, and exerted an effective monopoly in the manufacture of sewing machines. The general manager of the Kilbowie factory was an American, and he brought American technique to bear on the problems of improving productive efficiency. According to the workers, these changes resulted in wage-cuts, and early in 1911 a strike took place, led by the industrial unionists. The strike leaders published a manifesto which declared:

The international character of this firm must be kept in mind if we are to understand the recent developments. . . . Every device that human intellect perverted to the anti-social service of the enemies of mankind can conceive, is put into operation to increase the rate and intensity of labour and to reduce the wages paid to the workers. . . .

The strikers also complained that Singers were able to tide over the dislocation of their output by importing supplies from their factory at Elizabeth, New Jersey, and declared that "British labour is being defeated by American labour." They attributed this to the docility of the American workman:

Already these methods of capitalistic tyranny have been so successful in America that in many places no form of organization is possible. Over twenty years ago the great Steel Combine attacked the strongest Trade Union in America in the great Pittsburg strike and utterly defeated it. Since then in the whole city of Pittsburg all forms of labour organization have been remorselessly killed. Mr. Parks, the General Manager of the Kilbowie Works, wishes to reduce the British workers to the same level, to make Kilbowie, like Pittsburg, another "Hell with the Lid Off."[1]

The strike failed, and its leaders were victimized and dispersed; but most of them remained on Clydeside as a nucleus of discontent, and several of them were prominent in the wartime Clyde Workers' Committee. One of them, Arthur MacManus, was to be the first chairman of the Communist Party of Great Britain.[2]

Another important influence in the shaping of the movement for industrial unionism emerged at Ruskin College, Oxford, which had been established in 1899 for the education of members of the working class. The founder of Ruskin College was a wealthy American Socialist, Walter Vrooman, and one of its first lecturers was his compatriot and friend Charles A. Beard, who was later to revolutionize American historiography by his *Economic Interpretation of the Constitution*.[3] Vrooman however did not retain control of the college, which was managed by a committee of trustees appointed by the T.U.C. and other labour or co-operative organizations. In the course of a few years members of the college began to chafe under the restrictions placed by the trustees upon the character of their studies. Encouraged by the Principal, Dennis Hird, they sought to concentrate on sociology and economics from the Marxist standpoint, rather than to obtain a general cultural education on Oxford lines. A number of them formed an Industrial Unionist group to study the principles of the I.W.W., and early in 1909 began to publish a journal called *Plebs*, which reprinted extracts from the *International Socialist Review* of Chicago and from the *Weekly People* of New York, as well as reviews of books published by the American Socialist publishers. Prominent in the group were Noah Ablett, of the South Wales Miners, and George Sims. From 1908 Sims acted as agent for American Socialist literature

---

[1] *Socialist* (Edinburgh), July 1911. The "great Pittsburg strike" referred to is presumably the Homestead strike of 1892.

[2] Tom Bell, *op. cit.*, pp. 72 f.

[3] See H. B. Phillips, "Charles Beard, Walter Vrooman, and the Founding of Ruskin Hall," *South Atlantic Quarterly*, 1 (1950), pp. 186–91.

and was said to have boasted of selling £70 worth to the students of Ruskin College.[1]

Matters came to a head later in 1909, when Hird was asked to resign his position as Principal. With the aid of the *Plebs* group he set up a separate Labour College in Oxford, which was inaugurated by an address from the American sociologist Lester Ward.[2] The Labour College, shortly removed to London, was supported by the South Wales Miners' Federation and by the Amalgamated Society of Railway Servants, two unions which were to be the storm-centres of the "labour unrest." The college also secured subscriptions from individuals, including a number of American Socialists.[3]

With the yeast of industrial unionist ideas already fermenting among the Welsh miners and the railwaymen, there came a fresh impetus to the movement when Tom Mann, the great leader of the "new unionists," returned to England after a long sojourn in Australasia. Mann had already been deeply influenced by the ideas of the I.W.W. Jim Connolly had emigrated to America in 1903 and had sent Mann a number of pamphlets on the subject, written by himself. Connolly's view was that the I.W.W. was the successor of the Knights of Labor as the true expression of the American labour movement. Compared with these two movements, he believed, the A.F.L. was nothing but a "usurper on the throne of labour," and its period of supremacy was "but a brief interregnum between the passing of the old revolutionary organization and the ascension into power of the new."[4] Mann studied Connolly's writings with great interest while he was still in Australia.[5] On his return he decided to investigate the syndicalist

---

[1] G. Sims in *International Socialist Review*, x (1909), 158, and xii (1912), 674; F. W. Walker, *et al.*, *Ruskin College and Working Class Education* (Oxford, 1909), p. 12. The title 'Plebs' was taken because of the interest aroused by De Leon's *Two Pages from Roman History*, which was serialized in the *Socialist*, Dec. 1907 to Feb. 1908.

[2] "Education and Progress," reprinted in Lester Ward, *Glimpses of the Cosmos*, vi (New York, 1918), 331–40.

[3] See Dennis Hird's "Ruskin College Scrapbooks," Ruskin College, Oxford.

[4] "Industrialism and the Trade Unions," reprinted in J. Connolly, *The Workers' Republic* (ed. Desmond Ryan, Dublin, 1951), p. 81. See also R. M. Fox, *James Connolly, the Forerunner* (Tralee, 1946), chs. vii–ix.

[5] Tom Mann, *Memoirs*, pp. 239 f.

H

movement in France, and made a brief visit there with Guy Bowman, who spoke French. The French syndicalists possessed plenty of martial enthusiasm, but the state of development in French industry, which was on a much smaller scale than that of Britain or America, did not enable them to contribute very much to the theory of industrial unionism.

In July 1910 Mann with Bowman's aid began to publish a monthly pamphlet-journal, designed to fit conveniently into a pocket of the manual worker's overalls, and entitled the *Industrial Syndicalist*. In it Mann quoted the I.W.W. Preamble and spoke of the success of the strike it had led at McKee's Rock against "the notorious United States Steel Trust." He also quoted from a letter that he had received from Debs advocating industrial unionism.[1] Towards the end of the same year, however, Mann was criticizing the I.W.W. for setting itself up in rivalry to the existing unions. Permeation, he thought, was better than "dual unionism" (as the Americans called it).[2] To pursue this policy, Mann and his sympathizers formed an Industrial Syndicalist Education League, which set about the work of propaganda and was responsible for the establishment of a number of "Amalgamation Committees" in different industries—notably Building, Engineering, and Transport—to press for the formation of industrial unions out of existing craft or sectional societies.

The years 1911–13 form the period in which the unrest was most manifest. The greatest activity took place among the transport workers, where Mann was most influential, and among the miners of South Wales, where Ablett took the lead. In June 1911 Mann was in close touch with J. Havelock Wilson, who was seeking to reorganize the sadly weakened National Sailors' and Seamen's Union, of which he had long been the secretary. Havelock Wilson visited the United States in 1910 in order to contact the British transatlantic seamen in Atlantic ports there, and returned convinced that he could restore the union.[3] In June 1911 a strike began, and the new liner *Olympic* was held up at Southampton. The seamen quickly won their fight, but the

---

[1] *Industrial Syndicalist*, Sept. 1910.   [2] *Ibid.*, Dec. 1910.
[3] Mann, *Memoirs*, p. 256.

strike spread among all types of port workers, especially at Liverpool, where riots took place in August.

In the course of these port strikes the Irish Transport Workers' Federation was formed by Jim Larkin in Dublin and Jim Connolly in Belfast. Jim Connolly had returned from America in 1910 after seven years away from Europe. He was now publishing a paper called the *Irish Worker*, in which he printed an "Open Letter to British Soldiers." This manifesto was written by a stonemason, Fred Bower, who was born in Boston, Massachusetts, and who had been a member of the Socialist Party of America.[1] The manifesto, usually known as the "Don't Shoot" Manifesto because it urged the soldiers not to obey any orders to shoot at men on strike, was reprinted in the first number of the London *Syndicalist*, a paper which had replaced the *Industrial Syndicalist* as the organ of Tom Mann and the Industrial Syndicalist Education League.[2] The editor, Guy Bowman, and the printers of the *Syndicalist* were sent to prison, as was Tom Mann himself, who read the letter to a Manchester audience. The *Syndicalist* in the meantime would probably have died, had not Gaylord Wilshire, the wealthy American radical who had now become a syndicalist, stepped in to keep it going until Bowman was released. Upton Sinclair, who was also in England at the time, gave him some assistance.[3]

During 1910 and 1911 discontent had also been rife among the miners. In South Wales, where the ideas of industrial unionism had been spreading, a bitter struggle took place in 1910–11 against the Cambrian Coal Combine, a newly-constituted group uniting formerly independent holdings.[4] The unrest was at a high pitch when Bill Haywood, the leader of the Western Federation of Miners, the strongest union to join the I.W.W. at its foundation appeared in the area to conduct industrial propaganda and to advise on tactics. Haywood claimed later to have improved the miners' strike technique by persuading them to force even the

[1] See Fred Bower, *Rolling Stonemason* (London, 1936).

[2] *Syndicalist*, Jan. 1912.

[3] *Wilshire's* (New York and London), May 1912; Mann, *Memoirs*, p. 313. Wilshire continued his syndicalist activity in Britain, and articles by him appeared frequently in the *Daily Herald* and other journals.

[4] D. Evans, *Labour Strife in the South Wales Coalfield* (Cardiff, 1911), p. 3.

engine-winders to come out.[1] At any rate, the ideas of industrial unionism continued to make headway, as was shown by the publication in 1912 of *The Miners' Next Step*, a pamphlet written by Noah Ablett and others and issued by the "unofficial committee" of the South Wales Miners' Federation, whose address was the Plebs Club, Tonypandy. The pamphlet demanded more militant union leadership and a policy of centralization on industrial lines, and in this and succeeding years the advocates of this policy rapidly took over the South Wales Miners' Federation from the older, more conservative officials.[2] In the same year occurred a six-week national miners' strike, which Lord Robert Cecil, M.P., son of the great Lord Salisbury, described in the Commons as "part of a great conspiracy" aimed at winning "dictatorial power over the industries of this country by a small band of revolutionaries."[3]

The climax of unrest in Britain in 1912 coincided with the greatest success of the I.W.W. in America—the textile strike at Lawrence, Massachusetts, where Haywood and others assumed the leadership of the workers—predominantly unskilled immigrants—and, after a good deal of violence, won important concessions. G. D. H. Cole was not alone at the time in hailing it as "the beginning of a tremendous new industrial movement."[4] Hyndman noted with regret that "it gave a great impetus to the anti-political side of the movement."[5] Nevertheless, the I.W.W. was unable to consolidate its victories. The immigrants were basically conservative in their attitude to the institutions of their new homeland, and only desperate circumstances had driven them to revolt. As soon as they had won some concessions from their employers, they abandoned their newly-found solidarity,

[1] *International Socialist Review*, xi (1911), 682; W. D. Haywood, *Bill Haywood's Book* (New York, 1929), pp. 234-6.

[2] D. Evans, *op. cit.*, p. 201.

[3] *Parl. Deb.*, 5th ser., xxxv, 1766 (19 Mar. 1912).

[4] G. D. H. Cole, *World of Labour* (London, 1913), p. 150.

[5] H. M. Hyndman, *Further Reminiscences* (London, 1912), p. 344. Hyndman was faced with an awkward syndicalist revolt inside his own party (formerly the S.D.F., now the British Socialist Party), for which see H. W. Lee and E. Archbold, *Social Democracy in Britain* (London, 1935), pp. 183 f. The syndicalists were especially strong in the Birmingham area, as is shown by the "B.S.P. Papers," Brit. Lib. Pol. Sci.

and the I.W.W. was never able to sustain its challenge to the A.F.L. for what Connolly had called "the throne of labour."

Mann himself sensed that the policy of "dual unionism" would fail in America, and in 1913 he crossed the Atlantic to persuade the I.W.W. leaders to accept his own policy of "permeation" or (as the Americans preferred to call it) "boring from within." This naturally brought him into alliance with William Z. Foster, who had been led to favour the same tactics as a result of a visit he had paid to England in 1911. Haywood, on the other hand, disagreed and clung to the policy of "dual unionism."[1]

Meanwhile the Irish Transport Workers, whom Larkin was treating as a nucleus of the "one Big Union" on the I.W.W. plan, had become involved in a desperate conflict with the Dublin employers.[2] In the course of an eight months' struggle in 1913–14, Larkin sought help in Britain, and a strong minority of the British labour movement, with the support of George Lansbury's paper the *Daily Herald*, demanded sympathetic strike action. Haywood was again on the scene, having been invited by the editor of the *Daily Herald*, Charles Lapworth—himself the veteran of Socialist campaigning in America.[3] The Dublin strike collapsed in January 1914; and on the eve of the World War, as G. D. H. Cole has said, "the left and right wings of British Trade Unionism confronted each other fiercely over the grave of the Dublin struggle."[4] The ferment of unrest was still at work, especially among the miners, the railwaymen and the transport workers; and after the formation of the National Union of Railwaymen in 1913 by the amalgamation of three existing railway unions—itself an outcome of the

[1] W. Z. Foster in *Solidarity* (New Castle, Pa.), 4 Nov. 1911; P. F. Brissenden, *The I.W.W.* (New York, 1919), pp. 297 ff.

[2] W. P. Ryan, *Irish Labour Movement* (Dublin, 1919), ch. xvi.

[3] *Daily Herald*, 15 Nov. and 13 Dec. 1913. Lapworth had accompanied Debs on his "Red Special" railroad campaign in the 1908 Presidential election. Lansbury, who had joined the Industrial Syndicalist Education League in 1911, did not become the active editor of the *Daily Herald* until February 1914, when he returned from a visit to America. Lansbury's trip was sponsored by the Single-Taxer Joseph Fels, but in the course of it "Max Eastman, his wife, and colleagues of the *Masses* did all in their power to help us understand American politics and the futility of American labour bosses." [G. Lansbury, *My Life* (London, 1928), p. 104.]

[4] G. D. H. Cole, *Short History of the British Working Class Movement*, p. 348.

agitation for industrial unionism—the organized workers of the three industries united themselves in the Triple Alliance, whose object was mutual sympathetic support in the event of a strike affecting any one of the three industries. The outbreak of war prevented the alliance from being put to an early test, and the climax of sympathetic strike action, in the form of the General Strike, was postponed until 1926.

It remains only to consider Guild Socialism, which arose from criticism of the nationalization proposals of the Fabians by a new generation of thinkers influenced by the labour unrest and anxious to find ways and means of giving the workers the greatest possible share in the determination of their own conditions and methods of work. Guild Socialism was first propounded by A. R. Orage and S. G. Hobson in the pages of the weekly *New Age*. Although, according to G. D. H. Cole, another leader of the movement, it owed more to French syndicalism than to American industrial unionism,[1] the attitude of the movement to American industrial developments was definite and uncompromising. Orage and Hobson believed that America would easily defeat Britain in a struggle based upon "quantitative production"—that is to say, mass production: but this type of industry, organized by the trusts, resulted, they maintained, in the "neglect of . . . aesthetic, human, and spiritual values," and inculcated in the workers "the virtues of the machine."[2] The path for Britain to follow, both for the sake of her workers and in order to secure a reliable export market, was "qualitative production" of goods by Guilds with high standards of skill and with plenty of scope for the worker to exercise his initiative and individuality. The Guild versus the Trust therefore meant the Good Life versus Industrial Slavery. The Guild Socialists, like William Morris to whose inspiration they owed much, were far more directly hostile than the State Socialists to the growth of mass industry, which they all regarded as a distinctively American contribution to modern society: for whereas the State Socialists regarded the growth of mass industry with satisfaction, as a sign of economic maturity likely to hasten the revolution that

[1] Cole, *Short History of the British Working Class Movement*, p. 325.
[2] *New Age*, 17 Apr. 1913.

they desired, the Guild Socialists could only condemn it as leading to a further loss of the values which they sought to maintain.

*   *   *

It has not been the object of this discussion to attempt an assessment of the influence of American ideas as a whole upon the British labour movement, but rather to examine the attitude of British workers and their allies among the intellectuals to the economic situation in the United States. French syndicalism undoubtedly played its part, along with American industrial unionism, in shaping the manifestations of unrest in Britain: though the language barrier was too great to enable many workers to follow the course of events in France. Irish nationalism, too, played its part, as can be seen from the careers of Connolly and Larkin. Clearly, however, many of the British workers had arrived at definite views of the state of society in America, which affected their attitude to their own political situation. Across the Atlantic they saw an exacerbation of the class conflict and a deterioration of the condition of the workers, which they were determined to avert in Britain. The power of the trusts, the brutality of the struggle between capital and labour, the damaging effects of the "speed-up"—these impressions formed the main features of the picture of American labour conditions that they had in their minds, leading them in this period more than in any other to chafe at the bonds of Fabian gradualist tactics and mild reformism which had so far been the characteristic form of Socialism in the British environment. Among the permanent results of the unrest were the Labour Colleges of the inter-war years and the more strictly Marxist education which they provided for a large section of the working-class leadership. Although the S.L.P. and the other organizations of industrial unionism did not last for long, those who had belonged to them formed the backbone of the Communist Party of Great Britain at the time of its foundation after the First World War. Thus the ideology of the militant left in Britain, such as it has been over the last generation, has many of its roots in the interpretations of American society which were current in the early years of the century.

CHAPTER VII

BRITISH LABOUR AND PEACE WITHOUT VICTORY, 1917-18

THE outbreak of the European War in 1914 at once transformed the political configuration of the Left in Britain, and also altered its attitudes to America. The bulk of the Labour Party threw its support behind the war effort, but a minority of the Parliamentary group consisting entirely of I.L.P. representatives—the convinced adherents of international Socialism—opposed the country's entry into the war and worked steadily for an early peace. But it was not supposed that the war would last long; and such was the internal strength of the Labour Party at the time, and such the degree of understanding between Arthur Henderson, the majority leader, and Ramsay MacDonald, the leader of the I.L.P. group, that the ties of party connection were not severed, and MacDonald continued to hold the post of Treasurer of the Labour Party throughout the war. At the same time, in the task of anti-war propaganda, highly unpopular as it was in the country as a whole, the minority linked hands informally with a pacifist section of the Liberal Party. MacDonald cemented this alliance by joining with four Liberals—Norman Angell, E. D. Morel, Charles Trevelyan and Arthur Ponsonby—to form a new body, the Union of Democratic Control, the purpose of which was to agitate for peace negotiations and for the end of the secret diplomacy which was believed to have been responsible for the outbreak of war.[1]

In the first two years of the war, while the main bulk of British political opinion looked upon the neutrality of the United States with increasing irritation, the members of the U.D.C. naturally took a different view. They welcomed the American attitude or detachment from the struggle, and hoped in 1916 that it would be possible for President Wilson to act as a mediator between the belligerents. W. H. Buckler, an American who was a graduate of Trinity College, Cambridge, and who had been attached to the

[1] For the origins of the U.D.C. see H. M. Swanwick, *Builders of Peace* (London, 1924.)

United States embassy in London as a special assistant shortly after the outbreak of war, kept Colonel House, the President's adviser, closely in touch with the views of the "negotiation group" as he called it. Buckler had ready access to the group through Charles Trevelyan who had been a contemporary and friend of his at Trinity. He wrote from London at the end of 1916:

As they are so friendly to the President's policy and to our country their views may interest you . . . MacDonald and the others believe . . . that both sides ought to state terms privately and confidentially to Uncle Sam as the "honest broker."[1]

This was at a time when Page, the strongly Anglophile ambassador of the United States in London, was confiding to his diary the view that Wilson's "distressing peace move"—his last appeal to both sides in January 1917—was "utterly out of touch with the facts of the origin of the war or of its conduct or of the mood and necessities of Gt. Britain" and "brought us to the very depths of European disfavor."[2]

Page's view of the majority opinion in Britain was unquestionably correct at the time: but in the course of 1917 the situation was radically transformed, not only by the entry of America into the war, but also by the Russian revolution, which, combined with spreading war-weariness, gave rise to doubts, especially in the labour movement, about the wisdom of Lloyd George's policy of the "knock-out blow" and "no peace without victory." The overthrow of the Czar, involving as it did the emergence of left-wing parties into active political life in Russia, raised hopes of a revival of the Socialist International as an agency for the discussion and perhaps also for the enforcement of peace terms; while at the same time the entry of the United States into the war altered the status of President Wilson as a potential arbiter between the rival coalitions—although he endeavoured to reserve his position by not entering the alliance of Britain and France.

[1] Buckler to House, 27 Dec. 1916, Edward M. House Papers, Yale University Library.
[2] Diary, 16 Jan. 1917, Walter H. Page Papers, Houghton Library, Harvard University. Wilson's January 22nd speech to the Senate was republished as a pamphlet by the U.D.C.: *President Wilson's Message to the World* (London, 1917).

In the succeeding months the attitude of the "negotiation" group in England turned from confidence in American democracy to anxiety as a wave of war enthusiasm swept over the United States. The London *Nation*, which at the beginning of April 1917 declared that Americans had "viewed this conflict steadily through the medium of the one moral issue it has raised,"[1] at the end of the month was urging that

The supreme test for democracy in America will be the measure of her ability to stop the formidable backstroke of war on liberty.[2]

On this point Philip Snowden, the I.L.P. leader, was frankly pessimistic: "There is little reason to believe," he wrote in the *Labour Leader*,

that America will long remain actuated by the noble impulses which breathed in President Wilson's speech. There are signs already that war fever is raging in the United States.[3]

For the time being, certainly, it became difficult for the American government to make any progress with the definition of war aims. In June the Union of Democratic Control sent Buckler a letter for the President urging him to demand of the Allies a restatement of their peace terms along the lines of his own January 22nd speech, in which he had spoken of a "peace without victory." The letter was not received with much enthusiasm, and Col. House maintained that it was for the Germans to give their peace terms before anything else could be done.[4]

Under these circumstances the British Socialists, if not so much their Liberal allies, were eager to try the medium of an international Socialist and Labour conference. Arthur Henderson, who had entered the War Cabinet as Labour's representative, had been sent to Russia to establish personal contact with the Kerensky government, and he returned firmly convinced of the need to hold such a conference as a means of maintaining the Kerensky

---

[1] *Nation* (London), 5 Apr. 1917. For a fuller study of British Liberal and Labour press reactions to President Wilson, see Carl F. Brand, *British Labour's Rise to Power* (Stanford, 1941), ch. iv.
[2] *Nation* 28 Apr. 1917.   [3] *Labour Leader*, 12 Apr. 1917.
[4] C. Seymour, ed., *Intimate Papers of Col. House* (Cambridge, Mass., 1928), iii, 139.

government in power and preserving the link between the Western nations and Russia. As he later wrote,

When in Russia I became aware that so far as the Russian democracy was concerned they were determined to have a conference if possible, I decided to advise my Executive to send delegates.[1]

Henderson's advice to the Labour Party Executive did not, however, meet with the approval of the other members of the War Cabinet, although Lloyd George favoured the idea for a time; and in August after the well-known "door-mat" incident Henderson resigned from the Government and thereafter threw his energies into the organization of the Labour Party and the shaping of a policy to secure a negotiated peace. Lloyd George replaced Henderson with G. N. Barnes, the former secretary of the Amalgamated Society of Engineers, and the Labour participation in the coalition continued: but the fact that the most powerful and experienced leader of the majority group of the Labour Party was now estranged from the government had a profound effect upon the political role of the extra-Parliamentary organization of the party in the remaining fifteen months of war. Henderson, in control of this machine, came to pursue an independent foreign policy, the strength of which depended upon the importance of organized labour in the war effort and the recognition that, in view of the divisions among the Liberals, the Labour Party was the alternative government of the country.

The keenest advocates of the Socialist conference were, however, the members of the I.L.P. Early in August 1917 MacDonald, through Buckler, intimated to House his hope that the United States would show approval of the holding of a Socialist and Labour conference at Stockholm "either by letting [the American] socialists attend or by expressing sympathy with its Russian promoters."[2] MacDonald did not however seem to expect that this hope would be realized. In a memorandum which he gave Buckler, and which Buckler forwarded to House and House to Wilson, he said that he and his friends

[1] Henderson to Frey, 1 Oct. 1917, John P. Frey Papers, Library of Congress, Washington, D.C.
[2] Buckler to House, 8 Aug. 1917, House Papers.

. . . look in vain for indications that Mr. Wilson thinks this war will have to be settled by political agreement, however long it is fought, and are in consequence driven to the conclusion that the effect upon Europe of America's entry into the war has been to strengthen aggressive Jingoism and to set back the moral and political movements that had become so strong in consequence of the Russian revolution.

MacDonald also said that he was "amazed" at the American hostility to the Stockholm conference, having expected that

. . . America with its republican and democratic traditions would have stood for the rights of the peoples, and would have facilitated the clearing up of the issues and the removal of misunderstandings by direct democratic contact and exchange of opinions.[1]

It is perhaps doubtful whether MacDonald really was "amazed," for he had been in America at the time of the Spanish-American War, and had seen the sudden rise of jingoism there when hostilities began.[2] In 1917, the European nations had had three years in which to get over the first flush of enthusiasm for war; but the Americans were eager to prove themselves in combat, and full of the fervour of a righteous cause. Nor was there likely to be much sympathy among them for the idea of an international Socialist conference. The American Federation of Labor, under the Presidency of Samuel Gompers, had always resisted the proposals for political alliance with the Socialists; and the American Socialist movement itself, strong though it had been in the years preceding the war, had a high proportion of German immigrants in its membership, and was particularly open to the charge of treasonable action by preferring the interests of Germany to those of the United States. There was thus little chance of the American government permitting their Socialists to go to Stockholm, and none at all of public opinion favouring the move. Just to make certain, the Executive Committee of the A.F.L. took the trouble in October, 1917, to send the Secretary of State a declaration denouncing the proposed conference as "untimely and inappropriate" and "harmful."[3]

[1] MacDonald to Buckler, 17 Aug. 1917, quoted Allan Nevins, *Henry White: Thirty Years of American Diplomacy* (New York, 1930), pp. 343–5.

[2] For MacDonald's reminiscence of this, see *Socialist Review* (London), xv (1918), p. 312.

[3] Lansing to House, 1 Nov. 1917, Woodrow Wilson Papers, Library of Congress.

The hostility of the A.F.L. to any suggestion of negotiations with the enemy encouraged both the British and American governments to think of ways in which by an exchange of contacts the American labour leaders might stiffen the military ardour of their opposite numbers in Europe. The British Cabinet hoped that Samuel Gompers himself would visit England;[1] but the work entrusted to him by President Wilson to assist the mobilization necessary for the American war effort prevented him from leaving the United States for the time being. Towards the end of 1917, however, Gompers felt it a patriotic duty to do something about the position in England; for Wilson, alarmed by intelligence reports from London about the growing strength of the "peace by negotiation" movement, asked him to suggest some means "by which he could help to steer Mr. Henderson."[2] Gompers therefore invited G. N. Barnes, the new representative of Labour in the British War Cabinet, to select a delegation of British labour leaders to visit America.[3]

One labour delegation had already visited America since the United States had entered the war: but Gompers had not been entirely satisfied with it, although it had given much useful advice on the problems which confronted trade unions in wartime. Gompers had asked Lloyd George to send on the delegation his old friend W. A. Appleton, the General Secretary of the General Federation of Trade Unions.[4] Gompers knew, of course, that Appleton was hostile to Socialism, and had no connection with the Labour Party.[5] At that time, however, Henderson was still in the Government, and it was no doubt at his request that Appleton was not included in the delegation, his place being

[1] Barnes to Gompers, Oct. 1917, A.F.L. Correspondence, A.F.L. Headquarters, Washington, D.C.

[2] Wilson to Tumulty, a note on a Naval Intelligence report enclosed with Lancing to Wilson, 30 Nov. 1917, Woodrow Wilson Papers. Printed in Ray Stannard Baker, *Woodrow Wilson, Life and Letters*, vii (London, 1939), p. 386.

[3] Gompers to Woodrow Wilson, 17 Jan. 1918, A.F.L. Correspondence; G.F.T.U., *Minutes of Management Committee*, 15 Jan. 1918, p 2. Compers asked Barnes to send "true Trade Unionists."

[4] Gompers to Lloyd George, 12 Apr. 1917, printed in *Federationist* (London), Aug. 1917. The *Federationist* was the organ of the G.F.T.U.

[5] Appleton had accompanied Gompers on his tour of France in 1909.

taken by J. H. Thomas, whose views were closer to those of Henderson himself.

Henderson, however, had now left office, and his place had been taken by G. N. Barnes, who was much less scrupulous to see that the majority view of the T.U.C. was given prominence. The delegation which he chose consisted of right-wing unionists, and Appleton was actually selected to lead the group, although the G.F.T.U. of which he was the secretary was no more than a strike insurance fund to which few unions were affiliated. Appleton owed his position on the delegation, in fact, to Gompers's expressed intention to regard him as his own counterpart in Britain. This was not simply a misunderstanding on Gompers's part, although it is true that the G.F.T.U. was the only British organization affiliated to the International Federation of Trade Unions before the war. The fact that the T.U.C. had not bothered to affiliate to the I.F.T.U. cannot excuse Gompers, who knew well enough, by virtue of the twenty-year-old annual exchange of fraternal delegates between the A.F.L. and the T.U.C.—which he himself had sponsored before the Labour Party was founded— that the T.U.C. was the truly representative body of British trade unionism. The willingness of the T.U.C. to participate in future international activity had been declared by resolution at its 1917 conference, at which A.F.L. delegates were as usual present.[1]

Gompers's preference for the G.F.T.U. had already been indicated in earlier exchanges with the Labour Party. When Henderson invited the A.F.L. to send delegates to a Labour and Socialist conference in Britain in August 1917, Gompers in reply had demanded not only the exclusion of American Socialist delegates but also the inclusion of the G.F.T.U.[2] He also instructed the A.F.L. delegates to the T.U.C. in September 1917 to attend an Inter-Allied conference organized by Appleton.[3] And in January

[1] T.U.C. *Report*, 1917, pp. 70 ff.

[2] Paul U. Kellogg and Arthur Gleason, *British Labor and the War* (New York, 1919), p. 237. This work, though perhaps unduly critical of Gompers, is a valuable contemporary account of relations between the two labour movements.

[3] A.F.L. *Report*, 1917, p. 247; G.F.T.U., *Report of Conference of Representatives of National Federations of the Trade Unions of the Entente Powers*, Sept. 1917.

1918, just before the new delegation of British labour leaders left for America, he sent Appleton a cable, for publication in London, congratulating him on his participation in the delegation, and announcing the refusal of the A.F.L. to attend any international conference before the German people had "establish[ed] democracy within their own domain." He expressed satisfaction with the Lloyd George declarations of war aims and the Fourteen Points which President Wilson had just enunciated.[1] Wilson himself strongly approved of Gompers's message, which he described in a note to its author as "splendid."[2]

By the end of 1917 one of the objects which Henderson had sought to achieve by sending delegates to Stockholm—the maintenance of the alliance between the Western Powers and Russia—had been virtually ruled out as a result of the November revolution, which brought the Bolsheviks to power on a programme of immediate peace negotiations with Germany and Austria. In the altered circumstances, it was decided to hold a conference in London of representatives of the labour movements of the remaining Allied Powers. Henderson sent an invitation to Gompers to attend this conference, which was to be held on February 20th. The invitation made an important concession to Gompers's views, by accepting his demand for the exclusion of the American Socialists. Henderson's message was despatched on January 10th, and was to have gone by cable, but for some reason the invitation was only transmitted by surface mail and was not received in Washington until February 9th.[3] Meeting two days later, the Executive Council of the A.F.L. at once cabled a reply, regretting that time did not allow the sending of a delegation, but reiterating its hostility to proposals for a further meeting with delegates from enemy countries:

We cannot meet with representatives of those who are aligned against us in this world war for freedom, but we hope they will sweep away the barriers which they have raised between us.

The misunderstandings between the British and American

---

[1] Gompers to Appleton, 9 Jan. 1918, A.F.L. Correspondence.
[2] Woodrow Wilson to Gompers, 10 Jan. 1917, A.F.L. Correspondence.
[3] Labour Party, *17th Annual Conference Report*, 1918, p. 8; A.F.L. *Report*, 1918, p. 49.

movements were increased when the cablegram, on publication in Washington, was found to have had inserted in it the sentence (of which Gompers subsequently denied all knowledge): "American labor believes German influences have inspired the London conference and until this is disproved will avoid the conference."[1]

The absence of American delegates was commented on with regret when the Inter-Allied conference met in February, and it was decided to send a small committee to visit America and settle the differences and misunderstandings which appeared to exist with the A.F.L. Henderson attached particular importance to this proposal because he had great faith in President Wilson and was especially anxious to win American support for Allied labour action. In March he went so far as to tell A. H. Frazier, the American liaison officer with the Supreme War Council, that he was prepared to follow any course suggested by the President: the President had only to "signify his wishes," and Henderson would "endeavour to comply with them."[2] Wilson was flattered and intrigued but also somewhat embarrassed by the appearance of Henderson as a genie of the lamp—"I believe," he wrote to House,

. . . you will think it as interesting as I do; but I do not know just what reply to make. It opens, of course, a channel of influence which may upon some occasion be very useful indeed; but, if I meet Mr. Henderson half way and, so to say, get into confidential relations with Henderson, is it not likely to embarrass my dealing with Lloyd George and the rest of the Ministry, to whom Henderson is in opposition?[3]

Within forty-eight hours, however, Wilson had thought of something to say to Henderson in reply. He had received a visit from Gompers, who indicated his concern at the proposed delegation from the Inter-Allied Labour and Socialist Conference. Might they not destroy the favourable effect of the Appleton mission by revealing the strength of Socialism and pacifism in Europe? The delegation's views would certainly jar on public opinion in America. Wilson himself thought the idea of negotiations with enemy Socialists was "outrageous and fraught with the greatest

---

[1] Correspondence quoted A.F.L. *Report*, 1918, pp. 50 f.
[2] Quoted R. S. Baker, *op. cit.*, viii, 38 n.
[3] Wilson to House, 20 Mar. 1918, printed in R. S. Baker, *op. cit.*, viii, 38.

mischief." The message that he asked House to send Henderson was cautious and friendly in tone, but its import was clear:

Express my sincere appreciation of the confidence he generously reposes in me and say that I would like to convey to him the intimation that it would make a bad impression in this country if any group of men were to visit it who would be understood to represent a party, whether that party be national or international, the people of this country being just now intolerant of parties and impatient of special missions, and this quite irrespective of the welcome they might in other circumstances wish to extend to the individuals composing the group.[1]

What effect this message had is not evident. The decision to send a small group to America had been taken by the conference, and Henderson by himself could not rescind it. But, whether as a result of the President's message, or because of the knowledge that the Allied governments would refuse passports, or through fear of a boycott by the Seamen's Union, the plan for a delegation to America was dropped, and it was decided to have consultations in London with a delegation of the A.F.L. which Gompers had announced was to visit Europe in the spring.[2]

Unfortunately for the European Socialists, the subjects which these A.F.L. delegates were allowed to discuss were narrowly prescribed for them. Lansing, the Secretary of State, cabled Ambassador Page:

There is no purpose on the part of the American delegates to discuss the policies or in any way to interfere with the avowed purpose of this Government or of any Government of the Allies.[3]

The delegation, which reached Britain early in April, was led by James Wilson, President of the Patternmakers' League of North America, but its ablest member was probably John P. Frey, a close friend of Gompers, who prepared the report.[4] The group met

[1] Wilson to House, 22 Mar. 1918, printed in R. S. Baker, *op. cit.*, viii, 44; House to Frazier, 27 Mar. 1918, quoted in *Papers Relating to Foreign Relations of the U.S., 1918* (Washington, D.C., 1933), Supp. 1, vol. 1, p. 177.

[2] Labour Party, *17th Annual Conference Report*, 1918, pp. 8 f.; T.U.C. *Report*, 1918, p. 66. Gompers told Henderson about the impending A.F.L. delegation in a cable of 13 Mar., printed in A.F.L. *Report*, 1918, p. 50.

[3] Lansing to Page, 2 Apr. 1918, printed in *Papers Relating to Foreign Relations*, 1918, Supp. 1, vol. 1, p. 189.

[4] Frey's report is printed in A.F.L. *Report*, 1918, pp. 138–50.

representatives of the T.U.C. and the Labour Party on three occasions in April, but on each occasion the British leaders were
annoyed to find that the Americans declined to negotiate and
limited themselves to "fact-finding." "They sat like Sphinxes,"
said William Gillies, who was a member of the Labour Party office
staff;[1] and this attitude at the private conversations was the more
irritating to the British leaders because of the readiness of James
Wilson to declare at public meetings his hostility to any communications with the enemy. Buckler described the conversations
vividly in writing to House:

From the intimate account of Webb, Gillies, and Henderson, it is
evident that the Americans impressed them much as shrewd, intelligent
backwoodsmen might impress a New Yorker. Their point of view
struck the English as provincial, and the extreme caution with which
they declined to give any expression of personal opinion, but insisted
on reading long and tedious extracts from the proceedings of the
American Federation of Labor, savored of antiquated formality. The
English were bored with the views of the American Federation of
Labor which they knew beforehand. What they wanted was a free
exchange of opinion with the American delegates. As they put it,
"We outsiders know what resolutions amount to, and we wanted to
get at what the Americans really thought."[2]

The disappointment of the British representatives arose from a
number of causes. It was evidently not only Henderson who had
an exaggerated idea of the extent to which President Wilson's
policy agreed with his own: in March the Webbs had discussed
with Huysmans, secretary of the International Socialist Bureau,
and Felix Frankfurter who was visiting from America, the
possibility that the President might "join hands with the British
Labour Party . . . and instruct Gompers to link up with the
International."[3] If Wilson was indeed "the only head of state
from whom a just and democratic peace could be expected,"[4]
then representatives of the American labour movement should
a fortiori be liberal in outlook on foreign affairs. To find such
reluctance among the American labour delegates to enter into

---

[1] Buckler, London Notes for Week Ending 4 May 1918, House Papers.
[2] *Ibid.*   [3] B. Webb, *Diaries 1912–24* (London, 1952), p. 114.
[4] The phrase is Buckler's, interpreting Henderson, in Buckler to House,
4 May 1918, House Papers.

discussion of war aims was consequently the more disappointing. Their enthusiasm was reserved for the hope of military victory: they were, according to another American observer, "truculent and warlike,"[1] and their speeches were quite different in tone from those of the war-weary British. But the main trouble was that the American delegates were afraid to negotiate, not only because they were inexperienced in the technique of international conferences, but also because they were no more than the "carefully selected and instructed" agents of Gompers,[2] who had far more power inside the A.F.L. than any one individual had in the British labour movement. Moreover, they were in receipt of Government hospitality throughout their stay in Britain, and this limited their freedom of action in many ways. Ramsay MacDonald pointed this out in an article in the Glasgow *Forward*:

We have tried to give them a few facts to digest and to set into their sonorous professions of faith and their adjectives and adverbs, but the Government are looking after them pretty closely.[3]

At the same time, the British labour leaders were forced to recognize the fact that the Americans were all quite unwilling to think of peace except in terms of a military victory. "The American mind," said MacDonald, "is where the virgin war mind of our own man in the street was at the beginning of 1915."[4] Consequently, all the British leaders could hope for was that their own views would be conveyed to Gompers, and would dispel the the illusion, if it existed, that the Appleton mission had been

[1] R. S. Baker, Notes of 18 Apr. 1918, quoted in his *Woodrow Wilson, Life and Letters*, viii, 172 n.

[2] The phrase is Buckler's, from his Labor Notes for Week Ending 4 May 1918, House Papers. Many British labour leaders no doubt shared Margaret Bondfield's view that Gompers was "too much the dictator of the A.F.L." Buckler pointed out to her over lunch at the Derby T.U.C. that "as the creator of his Federation among men of diverse tongues unused to British-American methods . . . Gompers had to lead quite differently." (W. H. Buckler, typescript memoirs.)

[3] *Forward* (Glasgow), 11 May 1918. Barnes in a public speech described this remark as "a fair sample of Mr. MacDonald's characteristic crookedness" (*The Times*, 13 May 1918), but there was a good deal of truth in it: even H. M. Hyndman, about whose "patriotism" there could be no question, found it difficult to approach the delegation, no doubt because he was a Socialist—see Hyndman to C. E. Russell, 24 May 1918, Russell Papers, Library of Congress.

[4] *Forward*, 11 May 1918.

representative of the British movement. They were at pains to point out to the Americans that although President Wilson had liberal war aims in view, the British and French Governments did not share them: "the American delegates should appreciate this important distinction."[1] This was a principal reason in favour of an international conference of Labour and Socialist representatives. The British leaders were pleased to know that Gompers was at least in favour of a Labour conference to meet concurrently with the main peace conference at the end of the war: they argued that this would need careful preparation beforehand, which should begin as soon as possible.

In addition to attending these conversations, members of the American delegation addressed a number of meetings up and down the country for the purpose of maintaining morale on the British home front. This, indeed, was the first object of their mission. Appleton was in charge of the arrangements for these meetings, and although a visit to Bristol had to be cancelled owing to the opposition of a prominent local union leader, Ernest Bevin, Appleton was satisfied at the end of the tour that "a great blow has been struck at our own Defeatists."[2]

The mission then went on to visit France, and returned to England in May only for a brief stay before embarking on the Atlantic journey. On May 17th they again met representatives of the T.U.C. and the Labour Party, and on this occasion they were presented with a T.U.C. document which showed that while the affiliated union membership of the T.U.C. and the Labour Party was 3,677,000 and 2,415,000 respectively, the affiliated membership of the G.F.T.U. was but 796,130, of whom only 81,000 were not also affiliated to either the T.U.C. or the Labour Party.[3]

But the delegation had made no concessions in negotiation, and there was no evidence that they had been impressed by what they had learned from the T.U.C. and the Labour Party. Their strict observance of Gompers's instructions earned them the highest praise of the conservative Ambassador Page, who described them

[1] Buckler's Labor Notes, loc. cit.
[2] Appleton to Gompers, 15 May 1918, A.F.L. Correspondence. Bevin's attitude was of special significance, for he had been one of the T.U.C.'s two fraternal delegates to the 1915 A.F.L. convention.
[3] Labour Party 18th Annual Conference Report (1918), p. 10.

in a letter to House as "admirable representatives of the bone and sinew of American manhood."[1] It was only through contacts lower down in the diplomatic hierarchy that House learnt of less favourable reactions. Buckler wrote that Sidney Webb had expressed to him

. . . the opinion that in the interests of allied unity it would not be desirable that any more American labor delegates, preaching the doctrine of the "Knock-out Blow" and of complete non-intercourse with German Socialists, should come to this country or to France at the present time.[2]

And MacDonald wrote to the secretary of the American Socialist Party to say that the delegation had

. . . convinced most of the Labour leaders here, irrespective of their views upon national policy at the present moment, that the American Federation is hopelessly out of date and has no grasp of the realities of European politics.

MacDonald described the delegation as "a profound disappointment" and spoke of their interviews with the American press on their return as "grotesque in the extreme." He said that the Labour Party was now faced with the alternatives of tortuously negotiating with the A.F.L. and ignoring European affairs, or of dealing with developments in Europe and ignoring the A.F.L. The latter, it seemed to him, was the policy they would have to adopt,

. . . although I regret it very much as I wished to see American labour and Socialism march along with us and help us to secure after this war democratic freedom and permanent peace.

MacDonald ascribed this situation largely to the Labour Party's decision (with which he implied personal disagreement) to ignore the American Socialist Party, in order to secure the co-operation of the A.F.L.[3]

[1] Page to House, 27 May 1918, printed in Burton J. Hendrick, *Life and Letters of W. H. Page* (London, 1924), ii, 387. Page, a publisher by profession, had been regarded as an enemy of organized labour before the war, and the London Trades Council had received the thanks of the American Bookbinders for protesting against his nomination as ambassador in 1913 (*London Trades Council History* (London, 1950), p. 100).

[2] Buckler to House, 18 June 1918, House Papers.

[3] MacDonald to Adolph Germer, 5 June 1918, Socialist Party Papers, Duke University, N.C.

Henderson also felt that the plans for contacts with Socialists of enemy countries should go ahead in spite of American disagreement; but he had not abandoned all hope of coming to terms with the A.F.L.[1] When Gompers announced his intention to visit Britain in person and to attend the Inter-Allied Conference of Labour and Socialist Parties at London in September, it was clear that a chance of agreement still existed. The obstacles to be overcome were considerable, and the prospects of overcoming them were not improved by the British Government's refusal of passports to the two T.U.C. fraternal delegates to the 1918 A.F.L. convention in June.[2] One of the delegates was to have been Margaret Bondfield, who was not only a prominent unionist but also a leader of the I.L.P. She would no doubt have been able to give a clear exposition of the views of the British labour movement, as in fact she did at the A.F.L. convention the following year which she was permitted to attend; but for the present, probably to Gompers's private satisfaction, the A.F.L. were prevented from hearing her statement of the position. Henderson wrote a "Letter to American Workers" which was published in the September *Atlantic Monthly*:[3] but this was hardly an adequate substitute for a visiting delegation.

Gompers announced his intention to visit England in a cable to Appleton on August 7th, and there followed a struggle between Appleton and C. W. Bowerman of the T.U.C. to determine which organizations should meet Gompers as the representatives of British Labour.[4] Bowerman declared that the T.U.C. proposed to join with the Labour Party in convening a conference to meet Gompers and the other members of his delegation. Appleton invited Gompers to meetings with the G.F.T.U., and complained publicly of the participation of the Labour Party in the rival reception.[5] Since Appleton was known to be closely in touch

[1] Buckler to House, 1 June 1918, House Papers.
[2] Gompers claimed that he had tried to get the passports issued—A.F.L. *Report*, 1918, pp. 276 f.
[3] *Atlantic Monthly*, cxxii (1918), pp. 300–3.
[4] Appleton in *Globe*, 15 Aug. 1918, commenting on an article by C. W. Bowerman in the *Daily News* of the same date.
[5] For Appleton's account of this, see his letter to Gompers, 21 Aug. 1918, A.F.L. Correspondence.

with Gompers, this aroused fresh concern in London about how Gompers would act on his arrival. Buckler reported the fear that the visit might be used "for the purpose of belittling labor by attempting to discredit the Executive Committee of the Labor Party and the Parliamentary Committee of the Trade Union Congress."[1] Even the Foreign Office, in the person of Lord Eustace Percy, began to worry about possible repercussions, and Buckler was told that Gompers would be received "as a representative of labour and not as a member of the Government." Buckler also reported that

. . . the Northcliffe and Beaverbrook press had been privately warned not to indulge during Mr. Gompers's visit in the expressions of ecclesiastical approval which they have used on several occasions recently.[2]

Henderson, however, naturally remained anxious about the situation, especially in view of Gompers's habit of addressing communications not to him but to Appleton and Bowerman. Buckler remarked of Henderson that

. . . there can be little doubt that he fears the result of Gompers's visit and that if Gompers assumes a position of hostility to him and his associates in the Labour Party, Henderson is likely to retaliate so far as possible.[3]

Nor was Buckler alone in warning House of the dangers of the Gompers visit. Ray Stannard Baker, the journalist, had been sent to Europe early in the year as a special commissioner of the State Department, and in a report which House sent on to the President he described the increase of labour unrest in Britain and France and commented:

If the more conservative leaders cannot control these masses of workers one wonders what effect Mr. Gompers will have on the movement! A great deal of unrest and war-weariness exists, which we in America, coming into the war with fresh enthusiasm, find it difficult to understand. To bring these men only a message of interminable war, for no clearly democratic or socially reconstructive purpose, as Gompers with the best intentions in the world will probably do, is not very promising.[4]

[1] Buckler to House, 24 Aug. 1918, House Papers.   [2] *Ibid.*   [3] *Ibid.*
[4] Baker to House, 19 Aug. 1918, enclosed with House to Wilson, 3 Sept. 1918, Woodrow Wilson Papers. For Baker's reminiscences of British Liberal and Labour politics in 1918, see his *American Chronicle* (New York, 1945).

Baker warned House of the rising criticism of America which he found among the Labour and Liberal groups, who "when I first came here in March and for two or three months afterwards . . . were strongly with us"; and House in turn warned the President:

I have a feeling that you are not so strong among labor circles of either France or England as you were a few months ago.[1]

Gompers duly arrived in England, accompanied by a small group of A.F.L. colleagues, and proceeded first to the annual congress of the T.U.C. at Derby. While he was there he met Henderson and MacDonald and found them "surprisingly cordial."[2] But it was the support which their policy had at Derby which made the greatest impression upon him. Gompers apparently decided then and there that it was no use fighting against the alliance of the T.U.C. and the Labour Party; one could negotiate with this alliance, and secure compromise terms, but one could not destroy it. The correspondent of the London *Nation* described how this occurred:

The very gesture with which he swept away a part of his notes, and announced that he was "shortening his line on the international front," was an eloquent testimony to the impression which the Congress had already made upon him.[3]

Later in the month Gompers and his group attended the Inter-Allied Labour and Socialist Conference in London which Henderson had arranged for them. Their very appearance at a conference which included Socialist representation was, of course, a concession on Gompers's part. But the conference had not begun before an embarrassing incident took place. The credential cards for the delegates were printed with the title "Inter-Allied Socialist Conference," instead of "Inter-Allied Labour and Socialist Conference." Gompers and his associates refused to sign their cards and were at first not admitted to the hall.[4]

[1] House to Wilson, 3 Sept. 1918, Woodrow Wilson Papers.
[2] Gompers to John R. Alpine, 4 Sept. 1918, A.F.L. Correspondence.
[3] *Nation*, 14 Sept. 1918. See also T.U.C. *Report*, 1918, p. 230; *Daily News*, 6 Sept. 1918. Gompers's remark came just after he had ventured to mention the G.F.T.U.
[4] For Gompers's account of this, see A.F.L. *Report*, 1919, pp. 104 f.

Once they were in their places it seemed that they were doing their best to dominate the proceedings. Bruce Glasier, an I.L.P. representative, described the scene in the *Labour Leader*:

Mr. Gompers was well planted in the centre of the hall. The chairman and the delegates could not escape from him. He smoked one cigar after another without ceasing even while speaking. He kept his hat on most of the time, and seldom troubled to take it off while addressing the Conference. He was master of the situation. Not a resolution or amendment could be adopted without his endorsement, and none which did not (if a pretext could be found) express acknowledgment to President Wilson and the American Federation of Labour.[1]

Mrs. Webb's account of the conference in her diary reveals a similar irritation with the visitors: according to her, they

. . . altogether outshone the I.L.P. in sanctimonious self-righteousness, and high-sounding declaration of ultra-democratic principles. They asserted and re-asserted that the war—at any rate since they entered it —has been a war between Democracy and Disinterestedness, on the one hand, and Autocracy and Lust of Power on the other. Whenever this thesis was controverted the Americans repeated their credo— more slowly, more loudly, and alas at greater length. "Are you stupid, criminal, or merely deaf?" was implied in their intonation, whenever the I.L.P. delegates expressed their pacifist sentiments.[2]

The American conference technique, however much to the distaste of the British representatives, was not employed without effect. Gompers induced the conference to hold its meeting in public and not in private, and thereby obliged Henderson, J. H. Thomas and other British labour leaders to adopt a more vigorous pro-war tone than they would otherwise have done. According to Buckler,

Had Henderson and Thomas not assumed a distinctly anti-pacifist attitude, they would have placed themselves in the foolish position of openly antagonizing Mr. Gompers, the ardent supporter of President Wilson whom Henderson and Thomas are constantly extolling.[3]

[1] *Labour Leader*, 26 Sept. 1918.

[2] B. Webb, *Diaries 1912-24*, p. 130. Gompers was evidently following the maxim which he later enunciated in his memoirs: "Socialists the world over are of the same mental caliber—there is only one way to deal with them— don't argue, just tell them."—*Seventy Years of Life and Labour* (London, 1925), ii, 438.

[3] Buckler to Irwin Laughlin (American Chargé d'Affaires, London), 29 Oct. 1918, copy in A.F.L. Correspondence.

W. Stephen Sanders, the pro-war British Socialist who was attached to the Gompers mission as a British Government agent, took the same view. Gompers's attitude, he said,

. . . undoubtedly helped to rally the anti-pacifist sections of the conference, who were much more vigorous than usual in the debates that took place.[1]

Gompers also received a letter of congratulation from the veteran Socialist H. M. Hyndman upon his "admirable stand."[2] Nevertheless, the Americans won no support at the conference, except from the Canadians and from an Italian labour group, for their attempt to defeat the plans to arrange a meeting with enemy Socialists.[3]

On the whole, both Gompers and Henderson were satisfied with the outcome of the conference. Both of them were realists, and both knew that it was essential for the British and American labour movements to come to some sort of understanding. Henderson had undertaken to ignore the American Socialists, and to accept the A.F.L. as the sole organ of American labour; Gompers had in turn recognized that Appleton's General Federation of Trade Unions did not represent British labour. Gompers had attended an Inter-Allied Conference which included Socialist representation; but he had maintained his refusal to negotiate with the enemy, and he had stiffened the declarations of the conference on the prosecution of the war. Henderson had secured an agreed statement of war aims on Wilsonian lines, and was still free to act on the majority decision in favour of discussions with the enemy Socialists. As before, the group which was most disgruntled by the performance of the American delegates was the I.L.P.: Mrs. Snowden said that the only satisfactory result of the conference was that "they had taught the representatives of American labour that they did not own the earth";[4] and MacDonald said that the A.F.L. delegates were "four years out of date, and on labour politics they were half a century out of date."[5]

[1] W. S. Sanders to G. N. Barnes, 24 Sept. 1918, copy in A.F.L. Correspondence.
[2] Hyndman to Gompers, 18 Sept. 1918, A.F.L. Correspondence.
[3] Labour Party *19th Annual Conference Report*, 1919, p. 9.
[4] Scottish Labour Party Conference, reported in *The Times*, 23 Sept. 1918.
[5] *Ibid.*

By this time, however, the German resistance to the growing Allied armies in France was weakening, and overtures for peace were made within a few weeks of the Inter-Allied Conference. Although Gompers's deputy at Washington, John R. Alpine, sent Wilson a telegram in October urging him to ignore these approaches and to "batter away at enemy lines until the road is cleared to Berlin,"[1] the overtures quickly led to an armistice on November 11th and the war was over.

★   ★   ★

The brief period of wartime relations between the British and American labour movements, which has now been described, illustrates some of the difficult problems which beset Anglo-American understanding in this field. In the course of these eighteen months it became clear that while British Liberals and Labour leaders alike expressed unbounded enthusiasm for Wilson's war aims, they were profoundly disappointed with the attitude of Gompers and the A.F.L. It is important to recognize that this was not just a matter of personality. The unfavourable impact of Gompers in Britain was due to major difference in the social and political structure of the two countries. Norman Angell, who was in America at various times during the war, wrote to the London monthly *War and Peace* in April 1918 to explain some of these differences, which he realized were likely to cause trouble. Although he was optimistic about the future of American Socialism after the war, he maintained that in 1918 it was largely a creed of foreign immigrants, and pointed out that it had little contact with "organized labour" in the United States, which itself was "confined almost exclusively to the skilled trades." Angell shrewdly observed:

I do not think that the real difficulties are in matters of international policy—though Mr. Gompers has based his objection upon meeting Germans during the war. The difficulties come from a wider difference of outlook and social policy.[2]

In fact, Gompers's objection to a conference including enemy representatives was based quite as much on the fact that it was

[1] Alpine's telegram is quoted in Arthur Willert, *The Road to Safety* (London, 1952), pp. 159 f.

[2] *War and Peace* (London), June 1918, p. 274.

to be a Socialist conference as on the fact that it would include representatives of enemy countries. MacDonald was aware of this aspect of the problem:

> The differences between us here and the American Federation do not originate in war policy, but come from fundamental diversities of attitude that have been intensified by different war experiences up to date.[1]

The fact was that Gompers in his war policy was carrying on his long struggle with Socialism—a struggle in which he had been engaged for a quarter of a century inside the American labour movement. The attitude of the British Labour Party, and the control which the Socialists had won over it, seemed to threaten Gompers once again with an enemy that he thought he had vanquished. This confusion of domestic and international issues affected his whole policy, and led him to make such undiplomatic statements as one at a New York reception for the British labour delegation in March, 1918:

> Neither Sidney Webb nor another Sidney Webb in America, could write the platform for the American labor movement.[2]

The same confusion was apparent in the minds of those who were his closest associates in England. Charles Duncan, for instance, a Labour M.P. whom Barnes had regarded as sufficiently reliable on coalition war policy to send on the mission to America with Appleton, announced at a public reception on his return that

> He agreed with the attitude and policy displayed by the American Federation of Labour in regard to the Socialist movement in the United States. The downfall of the labour movement in this country would be its association with the Socialist movement.[3]

Frey's report on the A.F.L. mission to Europe in the spring of 1918 made the same point. He advocated the establishment of a "purely trade union" international, and declared:

> It is unsafe and unsound to passively contemplate the influences exerted upon the trade union movement in the great industrial nations

---

[1] *Forward*, 25 May 1918.
[2] Gompers in National Civic Federation, *Addresses on the British Labor Party's Program of Reconstruction* (New York, 1918), p. 22.
[3] *The Times*, 30 May 1918.

of the world by political leaders, however sincere they may be, whose viewpoints and experiences are those of the theorist and politician.[1]

It is hardly necessary to say that these difficulties between the leaders of British and American labour did not end with the conclusion of the war. They continued throughout the peace conference and were a serious obstacle to the re-establishment of a permanent international organization of the labour movement. The feeling which MacDonald had expressed, to the effect that American labour was "half a century out of date," remained prevalent in Britain, and was only relieved by the hope that sooner or later American labour—if not the A.F.L.—would "catch up" and provide world Socialism with a leadership as daring as had been Wilson's leadership of world Liberalism in 1917 and 1918.

[1] A.F.L. *Report*, 1918, p. 142.

CHAPTER VIII

THE BRITISH LEFT AND THE NEW DEAL

THE aftermath of the First World War saw the political with-drawal of the United States from Europe. The Senate's refusal to ratify the Peace Treaty or to enter the League of Nations soon found a parallel in the sphere of labour politics when, in 1920–1, Samuel Gompers withdrew the American Federation of Labor from the International Federation of Trade Unions, which he regarded as too closely linked to the international Socialist movement.[1] Gompers died in 1924, but William Green his successor continued his policy—not, indeed, with much success in the immediately succeeding years. The membership of the Federa-tion, which had reached a peak of 4,078,000 in 1920, became stabilized at less that three million throughout the prosperous years of the nineteen-twenties.[2] "Company unions" run by employers competed strongly against the A.F.L. and helped to account for the large relative fall in its membership as a proportion of the "organizable" labour force from 19·4 per cent in 1920 to 10·2 per cent in 1930.[3] Still effectively excluded from the steel-works, the A.F.L. also failed to secure a foothold in the rapidly expanding new industries such as automobile manufacture and chemicals. The roll-call at its annual conventions seemed to reflect a decaying world of craft privilege: as late as 1932 the musicians' and the painters' unions were among the ten largest in the Federation.[4]

Another feature of the American labour scene in these years, as of American life in general, was the extent of racketeering, which was partly a result of the widespread illegalities arising from prohibition. To the European observer, used to the automatic

[1] Lewis L. Lorwin, *International Labor Movement* (New York, 1953), pp. 80 f.
[2] S. Perlman and P. Taft, *History of Labor in the United States, 1896–1932*, iv, 581.
[3] Figures quoted by S. Perlman in H. A. Marquand (ed.), *Organized Labour in Four Continents* (London, 1939), p. 404.
[4] Lewis L. Lorwin, *American Federation of Labor* (Washington, 1933), Appx. A, ii, gives the union membership figures.

discipline of "class-consciousness," it seemed that all vestige of idealism had disappeared from the American labour movement, and Mrs. Webb undoubtedly voiced a common British opinion when she attributed the "strange tolerance of bootlegging" to "the idealization, by the American people, of the motive of pecuniary self-interest."[1] Certainly in these years the average standard of living of the workers in the United States rose to unparalleled heights. Now that immigration was restricted, high wages and otherwise unbridled capitalism went hand in hand, and the supporters of laissez-faire in Europe pointed triumphantly to American prosperity as the justification of their faith.

The fact that New York, rather than London, was now regarded even in Britain as the main citadel of "international capitalism" was an indication of the rapid relative growth of American financial power during and after the First World War. The heavy cost of the war itself to Britain, and the failure of British industry to expand as American industry was expanding, enabled New York to replace London as the financial centre of the world. Substantial debts were owing to Britain from her wartime allies, as well as reparations from Germany, but her financial relationship to the United States was like that of other countries—all ranked as debtors in the American ledger. The inter-war debt question, with all the problems which it occasioned, did more than anything else to imprint upon the European mind that picture of Uncle Sam as the international Shylock which has persisted ever since. So far as the British Left was concerned, the impression was considerably increased in August 1931 when the Labour Government fell, so it was believed, as a result of political pressure from American bankers. It was true enough that the British Cabinet was informed that it could not expect a loan from New York without giving a guarantee to make heavy cuts in spending.[2] These conditions occasioned the crisis: and they were interpreted in the

[1] Beatrice Webb, 1932, in "Round the English-Speaking World," an unpublished chapter of "Our Partnership," Webb Collection, Brit. Lib. Pol. Sci. Bernard Shaw even suggested that while racketeering continued in America there was no point in repaying the war debt ("The Future of Political Science in America," *Political Quarterly*, iv (1933), 336).

[2] Charles L. Mowat, "The Fall of the Labour Government in Britain, August 1931," *Huntington Library Quarterly*, vii (1944), pp. 372, 379.

Daily Herald—now the official Labour Party newspaper—to mean "an attempt . . . to dictate the internal policy of Great Britain." The American bankers, said the *Herald* political correspondent, insisted on a cut in "the dole," and the reason for this was clear:

Behind the demand of the United States bankers lies anxiety regarding growing demands in their own country for the installation of some similar form of unemployed benefit.

Determined to make the most of this incident, a leader-writer described it as "a blow to British prestige equalled only in recent history by the terms of the Versailles Treaty."[1]

By this time, indeed, unemployment figures were rising even more rapidly in the United States than in Britain. The economic depression hit America with especial severity for a number of reasons: partly because of the excess of confidence which had preceded the slump, and partly because of the absence of any national system of social security such as the unemployed insurance of Britain, which, meagre though it was, undoubtedly did something to maintain the level of consumer spending. The ironic contrasts provided by the American collapse—breadlines amid agricultural surpluses, for instance—gave the critics of capitalism a fertile field for comment, and for several years they were able to make the most of it.

★   ★   ★

But if the depression caused the fall of a left-wing government in Britain, it also ended the era of conservative Republican rule in America, and replaced Herbert Hoover with Franklin Roosevelt. The new Democratic President was no doctrinaire reformer, but he had energy and courage and he realized that the situation required, above all, a fresh initiative. His New Deal was in the literal sense an experiment—or rather, a series of experiments, some based on mutually contradictory suppositions, but all attempted on the understanding that if they failed they would be abandoned. Many of the measures that Roosevelt took, especially in his first two years of office, were frankly restrictionist in character, and aimed at closing the gap between production and

[1] *Daily Herald*, 25 Aug. 1931. The argument was repeated in the T.U.C.'s official organ, the *Industrial Review* (Sept. 1931, pp. 2–3) by H. W. Lee, the former secretary of the S.D.F., who was now working for the T.U.C.

consumption by cutting down production. The two principal enactments of the early New Deal, the National Industrial Recovery Act and the Agricultural Adjustment Act, largely operated in this way; and although N.I.R.A. contained the famous Section 7(a) which legalized collective bargaining—a measure for which the unions had long fought in vain—in general its provisions were designed to enable business to recover along lines that suited business best. It was only after two years' experience, by which time the leaders of private industry had recovered sufficient confidence in themselves to start attacking the administration, that Roosevelt decided to exploit more fully the great volume of radical feeling which had been aroused by the continued existence of unemployment and poverty. The 1935 Congress passed, in most cases on Presidential initiative, a remarkable series of measures: the Wagner Act, which established the National Labor Relations Board; a "wealth tax"; a programme of work relief; and a Social Security Act. It was consequently with labour and radical votes that Roosevelt secured his triumphant re-election in November 1936.

In Britain, the cautious orthodoxy of the "National" Government's policy was in strong contrast to Roosevelt's boldness. The pathetic remnant of the Parliamentary Labour Party that survived the 1931 election—less than fifty members— could do little in the way of constructive criticism, and the Prime Minister himself, Ramsay MacDonald, was virtually a prisoner of his Conservative allies. What was supposed to be a "National" Government in fact turned out to be a government of the Right. From the first, however, it was not the Left but the Left Centre of British politics that gave the most enthusiastic welcome to the New Deal. Liberals, independents, and the more pragmatic trade union leaders all reacted favourably to this attempt to bring private enterprise and public initiative into partnership. "Planning" suddenly became a popular word among intellectuals of all types both in Britain and in America: it had been popularized in America by the "Technocrats," who avoided the issue of the ownership of industry while concentrating attention on the need for its public control. To those who accepted this need, the British government seemed painfully timid, by

K

comparison with Roosevelt, who even in his early restrictionist phase had no doubt about the need for vigorous administrative action.

Among the first to understand and to sympathize with what Roosevelt was attempting was the economist J. M. Keynes, who voiced the feelings of British Liberals in an open letter to the President at the end of 1933:

You have made yourself the trustee for those in every country who seek to end the evils of our condition by reasoned experiment within the framework of the existing social system. If you fail, rational change will be gravely prejudiced throughout the world, leaving orthodoxy and revolution to fight it out. But if you succeed, new and bolder methods will be tried everywhere. . . .[1]

Here indeed was an echo of Cartwright in 1775, of Bright in 1862, of Henderson in 1918, to stir and to challenge the new administration: but Keynes gave not only the warm encouragement of the European Liberal, but also the detailed advice of the economic expert. He criticized the restrictionist features of the New Deal, while praising the occasional recognition of the need to increase consumption along the lines of his own still unorthodox views. In the following June he paid a visit to the President in Washington. The interview was not very successful: according to Frances Perkins, the Secretary of Labor, Roosevelt later said of Keynes that "He must be a mathematician rather than a political economist"; and Keynes indicated that he "supposed the President was more literate, economically speaking."[2] It is clear that Roosevelt had little grasp of the theoretical side of economics and probably did not understand much of what Keynes was talking about. But empirical evidence and the growth of Keynes's influence among his economic advisers eventually made him, as Rexford G. Tugwell has put it, a "reluctant and inconsistent" Keynesian.[3] It is not

---

[1] *New York Times*, 31 Dec. 1933, quoted R. F. Harrod, *The Life of John Maynard Keynes* (London, 1951), p. 447. The article, with slight alterations, was also published in the London *Times*, 2 Jan. 1934.

[2] Frances Perkins, *The Roosevelt I Knew* (New York, 1946), pp. 225 f. The same passage indicates that Miss Perkins herself first learnt of the "multiplier" from Keynes.

[3] R. G. Tugwell, "The New Deal in Retrospect," *Western Political Quarterly*, i (1948), 383.

surprising that Keynes continued to follow the progress of the New Deal with rapt attention, and later gave detailed advice in personal correspondence with the President.[1]

Keynes had acted as economic adviser of the Liberal Party in the nineteen-twenties, and it was natural that Lloyd George, who still regarded himself as a candidate for national leadership, should look with favour upon the New Deal. Lloyd George was immediately impressed with Roosevelt's efforts, which many British observers were inclined to compare—at any rate in their reform aspects—with his own legislation during the years of Liberal Government before the First World War. Early in 1935 Lloyd George produced his own proposals for a New Deal for Britain, in which the American inspiration was obvious, although, as the veteran statesman was quick to emphasize, "American remedies are not necessarily applicable to this country." Lloyd George's plan included a substantial amount of public works, including a national programme of road-building, which would absorb the unemployed after the fashion of the Works Progress Administration. Lloyd George also noted with approval that the President, after starting with recovery measures, was "now proclaiming that a new order is necessary." The same applied to Britain, and Lloyd George's proposals included a reconstruction of the Cabinet system and the creation of permanent economic planning machinery.[2] Clearly, if America had a Roosevelt in command, Britain needed a Lloyd George. Unfortunately for the latter, however, the Government was strong enough to reject his scheme and shortly afterwards to win a fresh lease of life from a General Election which was largely fought on issues of foreign policy.

But the demand in Britain for strong leadership on the Presidential pattern was by no means confined to the principal candidate for the post and his personal supporters. In July 1934 a manifesto was issued by a number of prominent public men and women who later became known as the "Next Five Years

[1] See Seymour E. Harris, *John Maynard Keynes* (New York, 1955), esp. ch. 24.

[2] D. Lloyd George, *Organizing Prosperity* (London, 1935); his speech at Bangor, reported in *The Times*, 18 Jan. 1935; Thomas Jones, *Diary with Letters, 1931–50* (London, 1954), pp. 139 f.

Group." The membership of the Group extended from young Conservatives such as Harold Macmillan to trade union leaders like Arthur Pugh and John Bromley, both ex-chairmen of the T.U.C. It also comprised a large number of Liberals and other middle-of-the-road figures such as Norman Angell, Gilbert Murray, and Lord Allen of Hurtwood. The manifesto, which was "On Liberty and Democratic Leadership," declared roundly:

The familiar paradox of dire poverty in the midst of plenty presents the sort of challenge to capacity for national organization which President Roosevelt has accepted, but our own Government has declined.[1]

Trade union leaders had a special reason for welcoming the New Deal, for they judged it by its immediate attempts to raise wages, reduce hours and improve working conditions. At the first Trade Union Congress after Roosevelt took office, in September 1933, Walter Citrine, the General Secretary, moved a resolution on economic policy which criticized the National Government and then went on:

Whilst re-affirming belief that social ownership and control furnishes the only adequate and lasting solution to the problems, Congress appreciates the significance of the vigorous efforts now being made by President Roosevelt towards the stimulation and regulation of industry by means of the Industrial Recovery Act and allied legislation; it welcomes the recognition given in that legislation, and in the "codes of fair practice" promulgated thereunder, to the trade union policy of reducing working hours as a means of diminishing unemployment, and of raising wages as a means of increasing purchasing power.

Citrine's speech proposing the resolution betrayed the warmth of his interest in the American scene: "he wished they were on the spot to measure for themselves what was happening." Margaret Bondfield, who had been Minister of Labour in the Second Labour Government, was among those who spoke in support of the resolution: she had visited America earlier in the year and had found the A.F.L. much changed from the rigid conservatism of 1919, when she had attended its convention as the T.U.C.'s fraternal delegate. "She found to her amazement that a real revolution of ideas was sweeping through America, led by the

[1] Quoted in *The Next Five Years* (London, 1935), p. 318.

American Federation of Labor and supported by public opinion." The resolution was agreed to without opposition.[1]

Similar approval of the New Deal was to be found in the other, much less influential, national organization of trade unionism, the General Federation of Trade Unions, whose secretary was still W. A. Appleton, Gompers's old friend. Appleton continued to keep in touch with Gompers's associates in the A.F.L. such as J. P. Frey, and through them he got up-to-date information on the New Deal. In his report to the 1934 G.F.T.U. conference he wrote:

Great Britain understands the seriousness of the experiments America is making. Some of them will fail; some will succeed; but whether they fail or succeed, they provide data which other countries can very advantageously study.[2]

★   ★   ★

It is when we come to the genuine Left—the acknowledged Socialists—that we find a more critical response. This was the period when almost all Socialists were warm in their praise of the Soviet Union, which seemed to have insulated itself from the world depression by means of the Five Year Plan. The more Marxist the British Socialists were, the more they found to blame and the less to praise in Roosevelt's policy; and it was unusual to find supporters of the President even among the less Marxist. But the latter contained one distinguished name, that of H. G. Wells, whose mind was too original ever entirely to succumb to an orthodoxy. Wells visited America in 1934, and was pleased to find the country getting that "sense of the state" whose absence he had deplored almost twenty years earlier. The concept of the Brains Trust appealed to his rationalistic mind, and in an interview at the White House he sensed the President's receptivity to new ideas. Indeed, he described Roosevelt in the highest terms of Wellsian praise as "the most effective transmitting instrument possible for the coming of the new world order . . . as it were, a ganglion for reception, expression, transmission,

[1] T.U.C. *Report*, 1933, pp. 261–70.
[2] G.F.T.U. *Report*, 1934, p. 7; see also Appleton to Frey, 29 Dec. 1933, J. P. Frey Papers, Library of Congress.

combination and realization which, I take it, is exactly what a modern government should be."[1] Later in the year Wells went to Moscow and argued with Stalin about the merits of the New Deal. Wells said that it was "a profound reorganization, the creation of planned, that is, Socialist economy." But Stalin could not accept this very un-Marxian interpretation: "The Americans," he said, "will not destroy the roots of the anarchy which is inherent in the existing capitalist regime."[2] A year later, Wells visited America again: the early restrictionist measures were failing and were under heavy attack; Roosevelt had not yet developed his new, more radical plans; the Brains Trust was démodé, and Father Coughlin was at the peak of his rabble-rousing career. But Wells, naturally an optimist and very anxious that the experiments should go on, urged his American friends to retain a constructive attitude to the efforts of the President, who was after all "a recipient and resonator of all that is most soundly progressive in Anglo-Saxon thought."[3]

Among other Socialists who dared at times to expect well of the New Deal, the exponents of the "under-consumption" theory were the most prominent. These were the publicists who were Keynesian before Keynes, the most notable being J. A. Hobson, to whom Keynes expressed his obligations when he published his General Theory. H. N. Brailsford, the well-known journalist, was much influenced by Hobson, and dedicated to him a book on contemporary problems which he published in 1934, entitled Property or Peace. In this book he welcomed the New Deal as "a daring experiment in economics . . . the first groping attempt to make mathematics the conscious mistress of an industrial society."[4] Although he was not sure that it would succeed, he readily allowed the possibility. Writing in the New Statesman early in the same year, he said:

It will bring us the answer of history to the question whether a planned and ordered economy can be built on the foundation of private enterprise and ownership.[5]

[1] H. G. Wells, Experiment in Autobiography (1934), ii, 789, 797 f.
[2] New Statesman, 27 Oct. 1934.
[3] H. G. Wells, The New America: The New World (London, 1935), p. 94.
[4] H. N. Brailsford, Property or Peace (London, 1934), p. 112.
[5] New Statesman, 27 Jan. 1934.

This, for a Socialist, was the crux of the matter. Later in the same year, as the early New Deal flagged, he wrote:

After a year of the New Deal few of us retain bright hopes that it will achieve any high degree of recovery, and fewer still expect from it a salutary and lasting transformation of the American economic system.[1]

Hobson himself, now at the end of a lifetime of seemingly fruitless propaganda for the new economics, was even more cautious than Brailsford. Even in 1936, when hopes were rising again, he was doubtful whether the President could achieve much in view of constitutional difficulties and "the unwillingness to extend the domain of public policy in the economic field." Hobson now thought that it would be necessary to nationalize a large section of industry if public control of the economy was to be effective; and to secure this object, he looked to the rapidly growing industrial unions, led by John L. Lewis, which he considered might become "the backbone of a new political party."[2]

If these two able publicists, who understood the nature of the economic problems that faced Roosevelt, were on balance inclined to pessimism, the bulk of the Labour Party appeared to be frankly hostile to anything short of a clear-cut Socialist revolution. With their backs to the wall after the crushing defeat of 1931, the members of the Labour Party often took an unusually bitter and dogmatic view of the political future, which was well expressed by Ted Williams, M.P., a South Wales miner and Labour College man, in a Commons debate on economic policy in late 1934:

President Roosevelt is trying by a system of planning, by schemes and by application of politics to economics, to bring to the people of that country the products of industry. We from these benches say that it is quite impossible for the problem to be solved unless he takes complete control of the industries and of the financial machine— complete control of the means of production.[3]

The same sharp distinction between drastic Socialism, which alone would be of use, and all other policies, was frequently

[1] *New Statesman*, 12 May 1934.
[2] *Contemporary Review*, cl (1936), pp. 653 f.
[3] *Parl. Deb.*, 5th ser., ccxcv, 457 (3 Nov. 1934).

voiced by members of the Labour Party in this period of disillusion after the defeat of their minority government of 1929–31. Thus the young Arthur Henderson, who like his father was one of the more moderate members of the party, could write on his return from a visit to America in 1933:

> Mr. Roosevelt does not go beyond the control of industry, and, assuring as it does continuous profits to the present owners of industry, at the most brings us on the road to state capitalism.

And for members of the Labour Party, he implied, state capitalism was no better than unrestricted private enterprise.[1]

If such was the situation in America, it followed that little of value could be accomplished without a strong Socialist party to bring it about. Attention was therefore focused on the prospects of the Socialist Party of America, and on the possibility of the creation of a Labour Party on the British pattern. British observers often sought a parallel between contemporary American politics and those of late nineteenth-century Britain, before the advent of the Labour Party. The implication was that the United States would soon reach the position of Britain in 1900, and so would feel the need for a Labour Party. What gave some force to this wishful thinking was the growth of industrial unionism which culminated in the establishment of the Congress of Industrial Organizations (C.I.O.). There seemed to be an analogy between the C.I.O. and the "new unionist" movement in Britain in 1888–91. It was a natural step to assume that this would lead to independent political action by American labour, for the "new unions" had taken the most active part, on the union side, in the creation of the British Labour Party. It is true that in New York an American Labor Party was formed in these years, with union support; but New York was unique in many ways. Mark Starr, a former Labour College lecturer and Labour Party parliamentary candidate who emigrated to America and became educational director of the International Ladies' Garment Workers—one of the most left-wing of American unions, largely concentrated in the New York area—frequently wrote for the British Socialist press describing the progress of the American labour movement. His British background and his New York environment undoubtedly led him to exaggerate the political militancy of American labour, and caused him to arouse unreal hopes in the minds of British readers. Thus after the 1936 Presidential election he wrote:

As the New Unionism of the '80's became the basis for independent political action in Britain, so the workers in the C.I.O. unions of garment workers, coal miners, radio, rubber, and glass workers will be the real support for "the new alignment" of 1940.[1]

British Socialists naturally accepted this view, and ignored the fact that American Socialism, so far from being on the upgrade, was actually the remnant of a movement which had at one time— before the First World War—possessed considerable strength. The usually well-informed G. D. H. Cole could write in 1933:

The day of American Socialism may not be yet; but in the light of the events of the past few years its coming may be much nearer than most Americans even now imagine.[2]

Two years later, however, he had to admit that

. . . at the present rate of progress, unless class-distinctions grow up with amazing rapidity, it will be years before it [the American Socialist Party] can hope to do more than capture a city here and there.[3]

The "progress," indeed, was in the direction of decay: even in the city of Milwaukee, where the Socialist movement had shown its greatest strength, the decline in its fortunes continued throughout the decade.

Whatever their illusions about the future prospects of American Socialism, British observers could see that it was still relatively weak, and they therefore concluded that the threat of Fascism in the United States was all the greater: the New Deal itself, it seemed, might be a first step on the road to the creation of a Fascist state. This possibility was taken with great seriousness, not only by the Communists (at least up to the time of the emergence of the

[1] Mark Starr, "Birth and Prospects of the American Labor Party," *Labour*, iv (Dec. 1936), 91. For other articles by Starr in the British press, see *New Clarion*, 24 Sept. 1932; *Labour*, i (Apr. 1934), p. 184; *Tribune*, 12 Feb. 1937.

[2] G. D. H. Cole, *Intelligent Man's Guide Through World Chaos* (London, 1932), p. 654.

[3] G. D. H. and Margaret Cole, *Guide to Modern Politics* (London, 1934), p. 159.

United Front tactic)[1] but also by many Socialists of the Labour Party and the I.L.P.[2] Their faith in the viability of political democracy, already shaken by the collapse of the second Labour government under financial pressure, received a further blow when Hitler came to power in Germany in 1933. Conscious as they were of the traditions of violence and corruption in the history of labour in America,[3] and influenced by the alarmist views of many American left-wing writers, they saw little reason to suppose that the United States would remain democratic while the rest of the world gave way to various forms of totalitarianism. The only question was—would America go Socialist or Fascist? For there could be no third alternative. In many ways the National Recovery Administration, with its codes and restrictions imposed by agreement of the employers, appeared to bear similarities to the "corporate state" of Italian Fascism. "From all the signs at present visible," wrote Jennie Lee in 1934 (the year of her marriage to Aneurin Bevan), "it is Fascism, not Socialism, which is most likely to overtake the American masses."[4] Miss Lee was especially annoyed by the T.U.C.'s enthusiasm for the New Deal: a year's experience, she said, would make the Congress resolution look "worse than silly."[5] Fenner Brockway, the chairman of the I.L.P. and editor of its weekly paper, the *New Leader*, visited America in 1934 to explore the same grim prospect of Fascism. He found General Johnson, the administrator of N.R.A., to be indeed an "industrial Fascist," and he concluded that the United States could expect a period of Fascist rule, to which the weak and divided Left-wing parties, and the conservative A.F.L. leaders with their enormous salaries, would be no bar at all.[6] Another Socialist who visited America in the following year was Sir Stafford Cripps, already prominent on the Labour Party front bench in Parliament. His conclusion was:

[1] See, e.g., R. P. Dutt in *Labour Monthly*, xvi (1934), p. 218.
[2] The I.L.P., which had become the refuge of the more extreme Socialists in the Labour Party, seceded altogether in 1932.
[3] "Brutality is usual in the U.S.A. It is so usual that one can hardly imagine the occurrence of an industrial dispute in which it did not play its part" (*Socialist Review*, v (n.s.), (Nov. 1933), p. 433).
[4] *New Leader*, 20 Apr. 1934.   [5] *Ibid.*, 8 Sept. 1933.
[6] A. Fenner Brockway, *Will Roosevelt Succeed?* (London, 1934), esp. pp. 232 f., 242 f.

The race for power between Socialism or Communism and Fascism appears so unequal at the present time, that, short of some miracle, the triumph of Fascism must be expected.[1]

Even a visit to the President in Washington did not provide Cripps with any optimism for the future of America: in a private memorandum which he sent to his father (Lord Parmoor) and to George Lansbury and C. R. Attlee, the Chairman and Vice-Chairman respectively of the Parliamentary Party, he wrote of Roosevelt:

My whole impression was of an honest, anxious man faced by an impossible task—humanizing capital and making it work.[2]

But the principal expert on American affairs in the Labour Party at this time was Harold Laski, whose influence at least on the intellectuals of the party was at its height. In this period Laski was never easily outdone in the forecasting of disaster. Keenly alive to the strength of anti-semitism in America, and worried by the growing power of movements like that of Father Coughlin, Laski in 1936 warned:

Let recovery be long delayed, let Wall Street make up its mind that political democracy is a threat to its empire (not as yet seriously challenged) and the next decade might see an end of historic America.

Laski combined these fears with an intense admiration for the personality of the President, and with a willingness to recognize the possibilities of the New Deal: "America," he said, "has a chance of showing that there is a genuine alternative to Fascism and Communism."[3]

Laski's ambivalent attitude to the New Deal, which is revealed in his many books and articles of the period, reflected the dilemma of a mind struggling to reconcile Socialist theory with the differing experiences of Europe and America. On the one hand, his affection for the American scene—devoid of many of the prejudices that affected other Socialist intellectuals—and his optimism for the future of a country which he always enjoyed visiting led him to expect well of the New Deal; on the other hand, his rigid

[1] *Labour*, ii (1935), 246.
[2] Eric Estorick, *Stafford Cripps* (London, 1949), p. 138.
[3] *Political Quarterly*, vii (1936), p. 464.

Marxist interpretation of political and economic trends forced him to conclude that the hope must fail.[1] At first it was the latter standpoint which seemed predominant in his utterances. Thus in *Democracy in Crisis*, a series of lectures prepared before Roosevelt came to power, he emphasized the Marxist view (not the less Marxist for having been shared by many American historians) that:

Once the last frontier had been crossed, it became the obvious destiny of America to repeat the classic evolution of European capitalism in a more intense form.[2]

This interpretation led him specifically to reject two years later the view of those who like Keynes

assume the possibility of a *via media* between capitalism and socialism directed by the state in the interest of the whole community, but without any change in the essential structure of class-relations.[3]

Yet by 1938 he was saying that

If our age emerges satisfactorily from this period of blood and war, I believe that the Roosevelt experiment in America, with all its blunders and follies, will be regarded by the historian as having made a supreme contribution to the cause of freedom.[4]

Laski was by this time in intimate and cordial correspondence with the President, and arranged to dedicate to him his forthcoming book, *The American Presidency*.[5]

What had caused this change in Laski's view? As readers of his final great work *The American Democracy* are aware, it did not last for more than a few years. The principal factor must have been his recognition of the fact that the President stood firm against the Fascist dictators, who now threatened the overthrow of all that remained of Western civilization. For people in Britain in the later 1930's the problems of foreign policy loomed above all

[1] For an interesting and detailed study of Laski's views, see Herbert A. Deane, *Political Ideas of Harold J. Laski* (New York, 1955). Mr. Deane does not always make sufficient allowance for the background of events at the time when Laski was writing.

[2] Laski, *Democracy in Crisis* (London, 1933), p. 44.

[3] Laski, *State in Theory and Practice* (London, 1935), p. 146.

[4] *University of Chicago Law Review*, vi (1938), p. 35.

[5] Kingsley Martin, *Harold Laski* (London, 1953), pp. 120 f.

else, and statesmen were judged less by their attitude to domestic questions than by their views on the Spanish Civil War and on resistance to Hitler and Mussolini. Perhaps, too, the disappointment with the Soviet Union after the purge of the Red Army added lustre to the rival experiment. But it was also true, as we have seen, that the later years of the New Deal showed it to be more radical than it was at first. The "Fascist" codes of N.R.A. expired when the Recovery Act was declared unconstitutional. Other manifestations of Fascist feeling, such as Huey Long's and Father Coughlin's agitations, did not last. The permanent results of the New Deal appeared to be "progressive": an enormous development of unionism, largely on industrial lines; the almost complete elimination of the "company unions"; a number of measures of social security; and some successful public works, of which the Tennessee Valley scheme attracted the most interest in Britain.[1] Although it was regrettable that the labour movement was now divided between the A.F.L. and the C.I.O.—the more left-wing British Socialists supported the latter, and were annoyed when Citrine sponsored the re-affiliation of the A.F.L. alone to the International Federation of Trade Unions in 1937[2]—still it was a matter of satisfaction that both wings of American labour were expressing themselves as strongly hostile to European Fascism.

Laski, therefore, was not alone in coming round to a more sympathetic view of the New Deal. Jennie Lee in 1939 stressed that "There are flags of freedom flying higher and wider in America than anywhere else in the world," and went on to the frank admission that after her numerous transatlantic tours—five altogether since 1931—

I totally failed to get any coherent picture of America. I don't think it can be done. And the more Americans explained America to me, the more blurred the picture became.[3]

Even John Strachey, who had poured forth Communist propaganda throughout most of the decade and had actually been

---

[1] See, e.g., Ernest Davies, "Regional Planning in the Tennessee Valley," New Fabian Research Bureau *Quarterly*, Spring 1938, pp. 19–27.
[2] For criticism, see *Tribune*, 9 July 1937.
[3] Jennie Lee, *Tomorrow is a New Day* (London, 1939), p. 162.

expelled from America in 1935 as a subversive agent,[1] by 1938 had begun to show signs of weakening in his hostility to the New Deal:[2] by 1940 his conversion from Communism was complete. The American situation was certainly not the only factor in his change of view; but there can be little doubt that in this case and in many others the New Deal played its part in convincing the Socialist toying with revolutionary ideas that there still remained a good deal of scope for the resolute reformer in the democratic tradition.

*   *   *

In the sphere of foreign policy most of the British Left took a more empirical attitude, at any rate so far as America was concerned, than the foregoing analysis might suggest. If the Socialists accepted the view, originally stated by Hobson but also argued by Lenin, that the policy of the great powers was dominated by the desire of finance-capital to find new markets, then they would be likely to expect Britain and the United States to come into violent economic conflict, eventually ending in war. Such a view was actually held by members of the Communist Party, who found evidence for it at the beginning of Roosevelt's regime not only in the debt controversy but also in the Ottawa agreements on Imperial Preference and in the conflicting attitudes of the two countries on disarmament and the Far Eastern question.

Nevertheless, the "rising Anglo-American antagonism" that R. P. Dutt, the leading Communist intellectual, confidently predicted,[3] somehow stubbornly failed to materialize; and those members of the British Left who were neither out-and-out pacifists nor committed to the Communist line demanded co-operation with the United States as one of the main guarantees of collective security. It became an established dogma among opponents of the National Government that Henry L. Stimson, Hoover's Secretary of State, had been anxious to join the United

---

[1] Strachey, *Coming Struggle for Power* (Modern Library ed., New York, 1935), p. vii.

[2] Strachey, "We Are All Reformists Now," New Fabian Research Bureau *Quarterly*, Summer 1938, pp. 14–25. See also his *Programme for Progress* (London, 1940).

[3] *Labour Monthly*, xiv (1932), 473, and xv (1933), 6.

Kingdom in active measures to halt Japanese aggression in China, but had been thwarted by the negative attitude of the British Foreign Office.[1] Throughout the succeeding years up to the outbreak of war, the left-wing advocates of collective security lost few opportunities of criticizing the Government for lack of enthusiasm in cultivating better relations with the United States. To be sure, no British Government would have made very much headway in view of the isolationist mood of the American people throughout these years; but the British Left was at least anxious that no obstacles should exist on the British side to closer relations between the two powers. Wells reported in 1934 that President Roosevelt seemed to be perplexed by the attitude of the Foreign Office;[2] and three years later Kingsley Martin, the editor of the *New Statesman*, wrote after a brief visit to America:

The lack of concern for American opinion manifested by the British Government amazes me. . . . The quality of Mr. Cordell Hull has never been appreciated here.[3]

In the autumn of 1937 the National Council of Labour (which represented the combined authority of the Labour Party and the T.U.C.) issued a policy statement on foreign affairs urging the closest co-operation with America:

There is reason to believe that, though American public opinion is largely "isolationist," President Roosevelt would welcome an opportunity of intervening to promote peace in any way that promises success. We should insist on the importance of promoting Anglo-American relations and making such an opportunity easy.[4]

Finally, in May 1939 the Labour Party conference in an emergency resolution on foreign affairs reverted to the same theme: it demanded

. . . that the British Government should seek and maintain the closest contact with the Government of the United States.[5]

[1] Mr. R. Bassett in his *Democracy and Foreign Policy* (London, 1952) gives detailed evidence of this view, which as he argues, was largely erroneous.
[2] Wells, *Experiment in Autobiography*, ii, 795.
[3] *New Statesman*, 10 Apr. 1937.
[4] National Council of Labour, *International Policy and Defence* (London, 1937), p. 6.
[5] Labour Party *Report*, 1939, p. 241.

In view of Chamberlain's astonishing rejection of an offer of diplomatic co-operation from Roosevelt in 1938—the incident which provoked Eden's resignation from the Cabinet—it would be difficult to maintain that the British Left's concern for Anglo-American relations lacked justification. It was significant, however, that this concern found such frequent expression among the British antagonists of capitalism.

★   ★   ★

Foreign affairs, then, obliged the Socialists to be realistic in their assessment of contemporary America. Whatever they thought of the future prospects of the people of the United States, at least they hoped to have them as an ally against the Axis Powers. But for some, there was a genuine appreciation of the merits of the American way of life, as adapted by Roosevelt; and many of these were thereby led to take a more favourable view of the prospects of democracy in Britain, and to await the accomplishment of such a "peaceful revolution" as that which was actually attempted in 1945-50.

CHAPTER IX

CONCLUSION: THE BRITISH LEFT AND AMERICA SINCE ROOSEVELT

AT the end of the Second World War relations between the British Left and the United States assumed an importance which they had never had before—not even in 1918, when Henderson conducted Labour Party foreign policy almost as if he were in office; nor yet in 1924 or 1929-31, when the party was in office but not in power. The period after 1945 had a special significance, for three main reasons: first, because the Labour Party was until 1951 both in office and in power—that is to say, it had a Parliamentary majority at its command, and could proceed to implement such measures of Socialist policy as it determined; secondly, because after the long struggle of the war years Britain was unable to overcome her economic difficulties without the help of the United States; and thirdly, because the United States, largely as a result of British weakness, was now obliged to accept the obligations of being the greatest world power, with interest in the affairs of all continents and with the need to sustain an active foreign policy by means of peace-time military strength.

The attitudes of the British public to American foreign policy in the years 1945 to 1952 have been subjected to careful and acute analysis by Professor Epstein, of the University of Wisconsin, in a recent study sponsored by the Center for the Study of American Foreign Policy, Chicago.[1] Since this work pays particular attention to the views of the British Left, which Professor Epstein rightly regards as having played the key role in the period with which he deals, it will not be necessary in the present essay to do more than summarize the outlines of the story, as a preliminary to setting it in a wider historical perspective, leaving the interested student to find the detailed evidence in Professor Epstein's pages.

*   *   *

The main problem of the period, so far as the British labour movement was concerned, was to reconcile the rank and file of the

---

[1] Leon D. Epstein, *Britain—Uneasy Ally* (Chicago, 1954).

L

party to the foreign policy of the Government which they had put in office. When he became foreign minister, Ernest Bevin rapidly discovered, in the face of Russian intransigence, that it was necessary for Britain to "negotiate from strength" if she was to maintain her position in the affairs of Europe and in world affairs generally. In view of the economic weakness of Western Europe at the time, this necessarily meant a close understanding with the United States—a "capitalist" power whose motives were, to the advocates of a "Socialist" foreign policy, either suspect or even necessarily evil. The Anglo-American understanding which Bevin nevertheless accepted as the basis of his policy took formal and permanent form in 1949 in a military alliance of the United States, Canada, and the countries of Western Europe, which now constituted the North Atlantic Treaty Organization. Although Anglo-American relations have since then been subjected to some strain, principally arising from the differing approach of the two countries to the problems of the Far East, the alliance with America remains, and is likely to remain, as the foundation of British foreign policy.

It is necessary to distinguish between, on the one hand, the supporters of the official policy of the Labour Government, and, on the other hand, the "Labour Left" who criticized the Government from the point of view of "Socialist principle." The former group, composed of the holders of Government office, the bulk of the Parliamentary Party, and the trade union leadership, has maintained control of the party conference, which at its annual meetings lays down the main lines of party policy; but the Labour Left, consisting of Socialist "intellectuals" and the bulk of the rank and file of the constituency parties, together with a minority of trade union leaders, forms a vocal and vigorous opposition element, though varying from time to time in composition, strength, and purpose.

Between 1945 and 1947 the Labour Left demanded a distinctively "Socialist" foreign policy, in accordance with the principles which the party had long advocated. Such a policy, they maintained, should be based upon the establishment of a "Third Force" of powers, led by Britain, which would be willing to combine political democracy with a Socialist economy. The

"Third Force" would be able to hold the balance between Russia and America, but would be independent of both. America was regarded as the great stronghold of private enterprise, on which the reforms of the New Deal had made little permanent impression. "America has swung right when the rest of the world is going left," said the authors of the pamphlet *Keep Left*, which expounded the "Third Force" idea.[1] The hasty termination of the Lease-Lend agreements in August 1945 and the hard bargaining of the American Loan negotiations later that year were regarded as evidence that "big business" was "riding high" in the United States.[2]

The policy of the "Third Force" collapsed suddenly in 1947 with the formation of conservative governments in France and Italy and with the generous offer of economic help for all European countries which was made by General Marshall, the American Secretary of State. The scope of the invitation, which included the Communist countries, and the fact that the assistance to be offered was for the peaceful purpose of building up the European economy, surprised and pleased all sections of British opinion; and the Labour Left made the discovery that there was more to America than "Wall Street," and that Truman, the Fair Deal and Point Four were not after all far removed in ideology from Attlee and the principles of democratic Socialism.

But this honeymoon of good relations between the Labour Left and the Truman administration was not to last. In 1950 the Korean war broke out, and the emphasis of American policy changed abruptly from economic aid to military preparation. The Labour Government accepted the need for heavy re-armament, but the Labour Left expressed misgivings about the new tone of American policy, and chafed under the extra national burden, which threatened the recently-expanded social services. In April 1951 Aneurin Bevan resigned from the Labour Government and at once assumed the leadership of the Labour Left—the "Bevanites" as they soon came to be called. In later years the cleavage between the official leadership of the party and the Bevanites continued, and for some time increased: it was probably an

[1] R. H. S. Crossman, Michael Foot and Ian Mikardo, *Keep Left* (London, 1947), p. 35.
[2] *Reynolds News*, 16 Dec. 1945, quoted Epstein, *op. cit.*, p. 42.

important factor in the failure of Labour to regain power at the 1955 election.

The Bevanites were critical of American foreign policy on all the major issues of these years: on the question of co-operation with the Government of General Franco, on German re-armament, and above all on the conduct of the Korean war and the non-recognition of Communist China. Just as, in the period of the Marshall Plan, the Labour Left had found ideological reasons for its friendship with America by emphasizing the significance of the Fair Deal and Truman's Fourth Point, and exaggerating the political importance of the American labour movement, so now the Bevanites justified their alienation by stressing the instability of American capitalism, the likelihood of an early economic depression in the United States, the influence of "big business" in the counsels of the Republican Party (which returned to power in 1952), and, finally, the irresponsible character of the anti-Communist "witch-hunt" which reached its climax under Senator McCarthy's leadership in 1953-4. By 1955, memory of the Labour Left's enthusiasm for American policies before 1950 had almost faded: as R. H. S. Crossman admitted in a review of Professor Epstein's book: "I had quite forgotten how enthusiastically pro-American the *New Statesman*, the *Tribune*, Miss Jennie Lee, Mr. Foot and I were in those far-off days."[1]

The official leaders of the Labour Party, committed as they were by their policy while in power, naturally tended to make more of the practical character of the American alliance and its advantages for Britain, than of its ideological implications. The alliance, they maintained, was necessary for the sake of the national interests of Britain: and their references to the question of Socialist principle rarely went further than to say that Britain and America could agree to differ on domestic issues. Ernest Bevin, however, and other trade union leaders, could justify to the union memberships their policy of supporting the Marshall Plan by pointing to the strong support that it was receiving from the American unions; and John Strachey, always a theoretician, could make a case for collaboration with the United States by arguing that recent changes in American economic structure had

[1] *New Statesman*, 9 Apr. 1955.

rendered obsolete the Hobson-Leninist analysis of capitalist imperialism.[1] Since they no longer formed the government, the Labour Party leaders gradually acquired freedom to attack American foreign policy, as well as British: but for the most part they used that freedom with restraint, and it was an exceptional situation which led Mr. Attlee in May 1953 to enquire whether it was President Eisenhower or Senator McCarthy who was more powerful in the conduct of affairs.[2]

The great wave of anti-Communist feeling which spread across the United States in 1950-4 was watched with considerable alarm by nearly all sections of political opinion in Britain. Probably the features which most aroused British concern were those which hit most directly at Anglo-American relations: the McCarran Act, which limited entry into the United States and set up an exacting procedure of examination for visitors and immigrants; the attacks by Senator McCarthy on British trade with "Iron Curtain" countries; and the extent to which the officials of the State Department, with whom many British people had personal contacts, were suffering from Congressional intervention.

It was, of course, persons of left-wing ideology who stood to lose most under the McCarran Act. The Act placed a veto on the admission, not only of members of the Communist Party—now a negligible body in Britain as in America—but also of former members of the party—a much larger group of politically interested persons who might, under favourable circumstances, have been persuaded to take a friendlier view of American society. The restrictions of the Act, by alienating still further this latter group, may well have multiplied the feelings of hostility to the United States which members of the Communist Party were invariably ready to exploit. The extreme Left now spoke of the revival of Fascism in America, and even drew comparisons between Senator McCarthy and Adolf Hitler.

It was significant, however, that the developments caused by the anti-Communist agitation in America in these years aroused almost

[1] Stable agricultural prices, a highly progressive taxation system, and the creation of a strong trade union movement were the points he emphasized in his essay in R. H. S. Crossman (ed.), *New Fabian Essays* (London, 1952), pp. 187 ff.

[2] *Parl. Deb.*, 5th ser., dxv, 1065 (12 May 1953).

as much concern among British Conservatives and Liberals as among Socialists. The "anti-intellectualism" and the absence of normal judicial procedure that characterized the work of the Congressional enquiries shocked the British public, and especially the professional classes, and it was the moderate *Manchester Guardian* and *The Times* which took the lead in expressing these feelings of antipathy. Even the members of the Left often reacted in a conservative fashion. Austen Albu, although a Labour M.P. and chairman of the Fabian Society, could write:

We all feel guilty about the British class system; but have we considered how far McCarthyism may be a product of the lack of prestige accorded to an intellectual élite in the United States?[1]

Indeed, it seemed as if De Tocqueville and Sir Robert Peel were right after all, and that the trouble was inherent in the nature of democracy.

British observers would perhaps have been a little easier in their minds if they had appreciated some of the basic causes of the phenomenon, which go far to explain its appearance if not to provide any sort of justification. These were: the exceptional bitterness aroused by the war without victory in Korea, with its relatively high casualties among American servicemen; the continuing feeling of frustration among a people which previously had been able to isolate itself from world affaris, but which was now carrying the burden of a global policy; the existence of strong anti-Soviet feeling among first-generation immigrants to the United States, who were also anxious to display their loyalty to their adopted country; inability to find a satisfactory definition of national loyalty except in ideological terms; the extraordinary perils of treason in the atomic age; the return to power, under a President inexperienced in politics, of a party which had been able to enjoy most of the irresponsibility of opposition for twenty years; and, finally, the division of powers between President and Congress which gives the latter the right of public investigation without corresponding administrative responsibility. If these causes—some of them transient factors in the American political situation—had been appreciated more fully abroad,

[1] *Fabian News*, Jan. 1954, p. 2.

foreign comment on the American domestic scene might have been a little less sharp, and the sudden disappearance of Senator McCarthy's popularity in 1954 would have been more widely anticipated.

*   *   *

In spite of these recent misunderstandings, there is evidence to suggest that the hostility to American politics recently so widely current in British left-wing circles may decrease in the future—assuming, that is, that no unexpected change for the worse takes place either in the economic situation or in the relations of the Great Powers. The elderly and middle-aged members of the Labour Party derive their most lasting impressions of American life from their earlier years of education and general reading, which in most cases lie more than a score of years in the past. Except for the most observant and adaptable of them, the America they know best is the "Land of Plenty" which belied its name—the America of the years between the eighteen-eighties and the First World War, when heavy immigration from Eastern Europe kept down the standard of living of the workers, and the British artisan preferred to return home, or not to emigrate at all, rather than to compete in so crowded a market.[1] This was the period which produced the literature of revolt, on which, with the help and guidance of the Labour College movement, large sections of the British working class have long fed their minds. The reminiscences of Aneurin Bevan will best serve as an illustration:

As I was reaching adolescence, towards the end of the First World War, I became acquainted with the works of Eugene V. Debs and Daniel De Leon of the U.S.A. . . . . When I found that the political polemics of De Leon and Debs were shared by so loved an author as Jack London, the effect on my mind was profound. Nor was I alone in this. My experience has been shared by thousands of young men and women of the working class of Britain. . . . From Jack London's *Iron Heel* to the whole world of Marxist literature was an easy and fascinating step.[2]

[1] In the thirty years from 1885 to 1916 the increase in real wages in the United States was only 7 per cent. (B. Weber and S. J. Handfield-Jones, "Variation in the Rate of Economic Growth in the United States, 1869–1939," *Oxford Economic Papers*, vi (n.s.) (1954), p. 124).

[2] Aneurin Bevan, *In Place of Fear* (London, 1952), pp. 17 f. Whiting Williams, author of an interesting diary of travel in industrial Britain, *Full Up and*

A generation earlier, the intellectually enterprising working man would read Emerson, Thoreau and Whitman: now, as the miner B. L. Coombes put it, he would devote his leisure from daily work to "hate in sympathy with Upton Sinclair, Sinclair Lewis, and Dos Passos."[1] If the prosperity and high wages of the nineteen-twenties suggested that conditions were changing, the calamity that overcame America in the depression at the end of that decade restored the stereotype. Although Harold Laski to some extent perpetuated the past by publishing in his *American Democracy* (1949) much obsolete critical evidence, it has become possible in recent years for a new generation of Labour Party members to take a fresh look at the United States and to form their views free from the traditional pessimism which, as we have seen, has coloured Socialist attitudes to America since before the party was founded.[2]

Since it is customary for the more Marxist members of the party to say that their criticism of the United States is nothing more nor less than criticism of "capitalism," it is also of significance that the present period of "Socialist re-thinking" is directing attention to the need for a reformulation of Socialist terminology and re-assessment, if not of ultimate ends, at least of methods and immediate objectives. "Capitalism" itself is now seen to have a variety of forms in different countries and at different stages of evolution. A body called the Socialist Union, consisting of a number of Labour M.P.s, and supported by members of the party leadership, has set about the task of re-educating the movement in these fundamental respects. In 1953 the Socialist Union published a pamphlet on foreign policy which boldly tackled much of the stale mythology still current in the party. "To dub Wall Street as the scapegoat for what is bad in American policy" was, they said,

Fed Up (New York, 1921), p. 202, remarked on the large quantities of Jack London's works being bought by British Socialists. Harry Pollitt, for long the General Secretary of the British Communist Party, once told Stephen Spender that he regarded *The Iron Heel* as the best revolutionary novel (R. H. S. Crossman, ed., *The God That Failed* (London, 1950), p. 238).

[1] *Left Review*, ii (1936), 829.
[2] See, for instance, the speeches of Christopher Mayhew and Denis Healey at the 1952 Labour Party Conference (*Report*, pp. 122–4); also, Roy Jenkins, *Pursuit of Progress* (London, 1953), p. 41.

a "childish over-simplification." They did not disdain the right to criticize the decisions of the State Department; but they argued that there should be less criticism than praise:

The U.S. has worked loyally within the United Nations; she has not been guilty of any aggression. There is no convincing reason for opposing this alliance on the grounds of Socialist principle.[1]

It may be, of course, that the intellectuals of the Labour Party will always retain something of the "holier-than-thou" attitude to America, which has been their inheritance, not so much as members of the Left, but as members of an educated élite which has no parallel—at any rate in its privileges—in American society. Originally, as we have seen, those who criticized American culture as materialistic and as leading to mediocrity of talent belonged to a narrow upper class, who feared that the coming of democracy would eliminate themselves from social leadership. Mrs. Trollope, De Tocqueville, and Matthew Arnold expressed this point of view. A comparable attitude is now to be found in intellectuals of all political persuasions, from the extreme Right to the extreme Left. At its best, as for instance in many of the reactions to the activities of Senator McCarthy, it is a genuine concern for the liberties of the individual, only too readily ignored in a mass society; at its worst, it is a dangerous form of social snobbery on an international scale. Bertrand Russell, aristocrat as well as intellectual, perhaps expressed something of both these elements when he said that in America "democracy is interpreted as meaning that the majority know best about everything."[2] The snobbery emerges most clearly in literary circles, and is more readily discernible in the pages of their ephemeral periodicals than in any of the political journals.[3] Cyril Connolly, the editor of

[1] Socialist Union, *Socialism and Foreign Policy* (London, 1953), pp. 27, 54.
[2] Bertrand Russell, "British and American Nationalism," *Horizon*, Jan. 1945, p. 19.
[3] See the discussion of the "Athenian complex" in André Visson, *As Others See Us* (New York, 1948). For an absurdly artificial attempt by the British Communist Party to assume the role of protector of British culture against American influences, see the *Arena* publication, *The American Threat to British Culture* (London, 1952), in which the principal vices of "Americanism" are listed as "glorification of the almighty dollar and of so-called private enterprise"; "incitement to racialism and hatred of national minorities"; and

Horizon, had no difficulty in explaining why it was that leading British writers like Aldous Huxley, Christopher Isherwood, and W. H. Auden had made their homes in the United States: it was, he maintained, because "the peculiar horrors of America . . . force the onlooker into a rejection of the world which might otherwise come too late."[1]

If such prejudices are inclined to linger, even to a limited extent, among the left-wing intellectuals, it may prove safer to look for signs of better understanding of the United States in the relations of the trade union movements of the two countries. Here, certainly, there is ground for optimism. After the Second World War, there was a period of some embarrassment when the T.U.C. and the C.I.O. were associated, together with the unions of the Communist states, in the World Federation of Trade Unions, while the American Federation of Labor preferred to stay aloof. In 1949, however, as the strain of the Cold War became acute, the T.U.C. and the C.I.O. withdrew from the W.F.T.U., and soon the T.U.C. and both wings of the American labour movement joined forces in the new International Confederation of Free Trade Unions.[2] Recent arrangements to re-unite the A.F.L. and the C.I.O. will undoubtedly facilitate closer relations with the T.U.C., and the influence of the somewhat more radical C.I.O. leadership should bring the A.F.L. more closely into line with the philosophy of the T.U.C.

British trade union leaders, being free not only of ideological presuppositions, but also of such social prejudices as might make them feel superior to Americans, have normally proved capable of seeing things as they have found them in the United States. The productivity teams which visited America under Marshall Plan auspices included strong trade union representation, and their reports stressed many of the same advantages of the transatlantic environment that their predecessors of the Mosely Commission

"worship of violence, brutality and gangsterism." The pamphlet provides a list of British authors who are supposed to represent the true national tradition: this includes Adam Smith and also, even more curiously, J. F. Bray, who was born an American and spent the last fifty years of his life in the United States.

[1] *Horizon*, Oct. 1947, p. 11.

[2] See John P. Windmuller, *American Labor and the International Labor Movement, 1940 to 1953* (Ithaca, N.Y., 1954).

had seen half a century earlier: an educational system which provides a "career open to the talents"; the respected status of technical training at the universities; the high degree of social equality existing between workers and supervisory staff.[1] A special trade union team which was sent to examine the role of American unions in increasing productivity strongly recommended that the British unions should "co-operate in the application of scientific management," which was a significant change from their negative attitude of less than twenty years earlier. This recommendation was undoubtedly linked with their re-discovery of the fact that "American workers exert no greater physical effort than their British counterparts."[2] Although the team recognized the differing character of problems facing the unions of the two countries, they nevertheless found much in American union practice to recommend to their British colleagues. The kinship of the trade union movements is a substantial reality to set against the will-o'-the-wisp of an American "Labour Party" which Laski was still pursuing in the last year of his life.[3]

As for the future of the British social structure, there are signs that a growing number of members of the political Left hold the view that the changes that they hope for will not simply be achieved by a transfer of the ownership of industry from private hands to the state, or even by highly progressive taxation. They are returning to the view of the nineteenth-century Radicals, that one of the most important obstacles to the creation of a classless society in Britain was the educational system, which perpetuated the existing divisions of society on hereditary lines. Gladstone's comment, they think, remains valid: "In England, inequality

[1] Graham Hutton, *We Too Can Prosper* (London, 1953), pp. 42 f., 122 f. The book was published on behalf of the British Productivity Council to sum up the work of the Anglo-American productivity teams.

[2] T.U.C., *Trade Unions and Productivity* (London, 1950), pp. 14, 60. For the view of the T.U.C. in the 1930's, see its report *Bedaux* (London, 1933), p. 16, which states: "So far as it [the Bedaux system] is a method of payment by results involving the timing of operations, it will doubtless continue to be opposed by the Trade Union Movement, as are all such systems." But the T.U.C. drew many of its criticisms of Bedaux from the A.F.L., which was also opposing it at that time.

[3] H. J. Laski, *Trade Unions in the New Society* (London, 1950), p. 102.

lies embedded in the very base of the social structure; in America it is a late, incidental, unrecognized product. . . ."[1]

George Orwell, an unorthodox but sincere twentieth-century Radical, stressed the importance of this problem:

No one should be "branded on the tongue." It should be impossible, as it is in the United States and some European countries, to determine anyone's status from his accent.[2]

Nor is this "branding on the tongue," and the other disadvantages that accompany it, now regarded merely as a source of social injustice; comparison with America suggests that the stratified character of British society acts as a hindrance to the economic progress of the country, by weakening the incentive of the worker, by limiting understanding between management and employee, and by leading to a failure to make the best use of available talent. There are, therefore, signs that Socialists are beginning to appreciate the importance of educational policy, and even that they are beginning once more to think that some lessons of value may be drawn from the American domestic experience.[3]

*   *   *

Inevitably, however, Americans must expect to receive criticism of their policies and actions from those brought up in different geographical, economic and social surroundings. The great influence now wielded in world affairs by the United States has forced upon a reluctant people the power to alter the lives of all mankind. It would be remarkable, therefore, if all mankind did not claim the right to comment on the decisions of the American government, and it would be equally remarkable if many misfortunes beyond the power of the American government to avert were not attributed, by those of limited understanding, to the

[1] W. E. Gladstone, "Kin Beyond Sea," *North American Review*, cxxvi (1878), 183.
[2] George Orwell, *The English People* (London, 1947), p. 44. It is interesting to recall that the author of this work, and also of *Down and Out in Paris and London*, was brought up in an upper-class environment and obtained his first impressions of the life of the poor from Jack London's *People of the Abyss* (Orwell, *The Road to Wigan Pier* (London, 1937), p. 172).
[3] See, e.g., Emanuel Shinwell, *Conflict without Malice* (London, 1955), p. 240.

failure of American leadership. This view is likely to be especially prevalent in a country such as Britain which can claim to have preceded the United States in the role of arbiter of world destinies. If it is true, as has lately been suggested by an American observer,[1] that the process of Socialist "re-thinking" signifies the "end of ideology" as a major factor in British domestic politics, it may be that the obvious differences between Left and Right over attitudes to the United States will increasingly fade into the background of a widely diffused national resentment arising from the relative decline of British power.

There is another factor, too, which inevitably contributes a special intensity to criticism of America by people of other countries: it is not the less significant for being, on the surface at least, in contradiction to the points just mentioned. It arises from the fact that the United States is by tradition not a nation-state but a community of people who have chosen to associate together and to dedicate themselves to a "proposition." The explicit idealism of the American constitution will always lead other peoples to expect much of the United States: the danger is that it may often lead them to expect too much. Herein lies the "irony of American history," on which Reinhold Niebuhr has commented with so much eloquence.[2] Hope and disillusion will long continue to colour the European view of America, as they did when Gompers crossed the Atlantic in 1909 to discover that people in Western Europe looked at his country as if in one of two distorting mirrors, either convex or concave.[3] James Russell Lowell had noticed the same thing forty years before: "for some reason or other, the European has rarely been able to see America except in caricature."[4] To understand the Americans as they really are requires not only an appreciation of the peculiarities of the American environment, but also a recognition that, in its better features and its worse, human nature everywhere and at all times is, as Thucydides said, very much the same. If the Americans themselves

[1] Edward Shils in *Encounter*, November 1955, pp. 52–8.
[2] Reinhold Niebuhr, *The Irony of American History* (New York, 1952).
[3] *American Federationist*, March 1910, p. 243.
[4] J. R. Lowell, "On a Certain Condescension in Foreigners," *Atlantic Monthly*, xxiii (1869), 89.

are not satisfied with this less than idealistic conclusion, as indeed the "Founding Fathers" were not, then they must realize that in the long run, the remedy lies with themselves, for, as Charles Francis Adams pointed out to Secretary Seward in words already quoted, and at a time when the United States was just half as old as it is now, "The progress of the Liberal cause, not in England alone, but all over the world, is in a measure, in our hands."

BIOGRAPHICAL INDEX OF BRITISH LIBERALS, RADICALS AND SOCIALISTS

Note—At the end of each entry visits to the U.S.A. are mentioned, so far as possible by date. Owing to lack of information in some cases, however, the list is not always complete.

ANGELL, (RALPH) NORMAN (b. 1874), author and journalist; managing director, *Paris Daily Mail*, 1905–14; helped to found Union of Democratic Control, 1914; joined Labour Party, 1920; Labour M.P., 1929–31; author of *The Great Illusion* (1909) and numerous other works. Engaged in ranching and mining in American West, 1891–7; a very frequent visitor to the U.S.

APPLETON, WILLIAM ARCHIBALD (1859–1940), Sec. of Lace Makers' Trade Union, 1896–1907; Sec. of General Federation of Trade Unions, 1907–38. Critic of Socialism and friend of S. Gompers. Visited U.S. 1918.

ATTLEE, CLEMENT RICHARD (b. 1883), ed. Haileybury and Oxford; Labour M.P. 1922–55; leader of Parliamentary Labour Party 1935–55; Under-Sec. for War, 1924; Chancellor of Duchy of Lancaster, 1930–1; Postmaster-General, 1931; Lord Privy Seal, 1940–2; Secretary for Dominions and Deputy Prime Minister, 1942–5; Prime Minister, 1945–51; cr. Earl, 1955. Visited U.S. 1907, 1941, 1945, 1950.

BARNES, GEORGE NICOLL (1859–1940), Sec. of Amalgamated Society of Engineers, 1896–1908; Labour M.P. 1906–22; Minister of Pensions, 1916–18; Minister without Portfolio, 1919–20; member of War Cabinet, 1917–18. Visited U.S. 1902, 1919.

BAXTER, WILLIAM EDWARD (1825–1890), merchant, ed. Edinburgh Univ.; Radical M.P., 1855–85; Sec. to Admiralty, 1868–71; Joint Sec. of the Treasury, 1871–3. Author of *America and the Americans*, 1855; visited U.S. 1846, 1853–4.

BEVAN, ANEURIN (b. 1897), miner, attended Labour College; Labour M.P. since 1929; Minister of Health, 1945–51; Minister of Labour, 1951, resigned after Cabinet policy disagreement. Visited U.S. 1934.

BEVIN, ERNEST (1881–1951), carter, later official of Dockers' Union; Sec. of Transport and General Workers' Union, 1922–40; Chairman of T.U.C., 1936–7; Labour M.P., 1940–51. Minister of Labour, 1941–5; Foreign Secretary, 1945–51. Visited U.S. 1915, 1922, 1926, 1939, 1946, 1949, 1950.

BONDFIELD, MARGARET (1873–1953), shop assistant, union official; on I.L.P. exec., 1913–19; Chairman of T.U.C., 1923–4; Labour M.P. 1923–4 and 1926–31; Minister of Labour, 1929–31. Visited U.S. 1910, 1919, 1933, 1938–9, 1941–3.

BOWERMAN, CHARLES WILLIAM (1851–1947), compositor; Sec. London Society of Compositors, 1892–1906; Labour M.P., 1906–31; Chairman of T.U.C., 1901; Sec. of T.U.C., 1911–23. Visited U.S. 1902, 1919.

BRAILSFORD, HENRY NOEL (b. 1873), author and journalist; ed. Glasgow Univ.; on staff of *Nation*, 1906–22; joined I.L.P., 1907; editor of *New Leader* (formerly *Labour Leader*), 1922–6. London correspondent of *New Republic* from 1915. Author of *War of Steel and Gold* (1914), *America Our Ally* (1940), etc. Visited U.S. on several occasions.

BRIGHT, JOHN (1811–89), mill-owner and Quaker; advocate of free trade; Radical M.P., 1843–89. President of Board of Trade, 1868–70; Chancellor of Duchy of Lancaster, 1873–4; strong supporter of North in American Civil War; opposed Home Rule for Ireland, 1886.

BRYCE, JAMES (1838–1922), ed. Oxford, Regius Professor of Civil Law 1870–93; Liberal M.P., 1880–1906; Chancellor of Duchy of Lancaster, 1892–4; President of Board of Trade, 1894–5; Chief Secretary for Ireland, 1905–6; Ambassador to U.S., 1907–13; cr. Viscount, 1914. Author of *American Commonwealth* (1888) and other works. Visited U.S. 1870, 1881, 1883, 1890, 1897, 1901, 1904; resided 1907–13; last visit 1921.

CHAMBERLAIN, JOSEPH (1836–1914), Birmingham industrialist, Unitarian; sponsor of National Education League and National Liberal Federation; M.P., Radical, 1876–86; Unionist, 1886–1914. President of Board of Trade, 1880–5; President of Local Government Board, 1886; Colonial Secretary, 1895–1903. Visited U.S. 1887–8.

CITRINE, WALTER McLENNAN (b. 1887), electrical trade unionist; Sec. of T.U.C., 1926–46; President, International Federation of Trade Unions, 1928–43; cr. Baron, 1946; Chairman, British Electrical Authority since 1947. Visited U.S. 1934, 1941, 1942, 1943.

CLARKE, WILLIAM (1852–1901), Radical journalist, ed. Cambridge; member of exec. of Fabian Society, 1888–91; contributor to *Fabian Essays in Socialism* (1889), on staff of *Daily Chronicle* in 1890's. Visited U.S. 1881–2, 1893.

COLE, GEORGE DOUGLAS HOWARD (b. 1889), author and univ. lecturer, ed. Oxford; Professor of Social and Political Theory, Oxford, since 1944; Chairman of Fabian Society, 1939–46 and 1948–50; President since 1952; leader of Guild Socialist movement during and after First World War; prolific writer on economic and political subjects.

CONNOLLY, JAMES (1870–1916), labourer, b. in Ireland, grew up in Edinburgh; member of S.D.F., helped to found S.L.P.; organizer of Irish Transport Workers Union, 1911; executed for his part in Dublin Rising, 1916. Visited U.S. 1902, lived there 1903–10.

M

HYNDMAN, HENRY MAYERS (1842–1921), journalist, company promoter and Socialist, ed. Cambridge; formed (Social) Democratic Federation, 1881; and thereafter engaged in unremitting agitation on its behalf. Visited U.S. frequently in 1871–80.

JONES, ERNEST CHARLES (1819–1868), poet and barrister, ed. in Germany; Chartist and Radical leader; editor of *People's Paper*, 1852–8; Vice-President of Reform League from 1865.

KEYNES, JOHN MAYNARD (1883–1946), economist, wartime civil servant, Fellow of King's College, Cambridge; cr. baron, 1942; author of important theoretical works on economics. Negotiated American loan for Britain, 1945. Visited U.S. 1917, 1931, 1934, 1941, 1943, 1944, 1945.

LANSBURY, GEORGE (1859–1941), timber merchant; member of S.D.F., changed to I.L.P. about 1903; supporter of women's suffrage and syndicalism; edited *Herald*, 1912–25; Labour M.P., 1910–12 and 1922–41; leader of Parliamentary Labour Party, 1932–5. Visited U.S. 1913–14, 1936.

LASKI, HAROLD J. (1893–1950), ed. Oxford; lecturer at Harvard, 1916–20; Professor of Political Science, London, 1926–50; member of Labour Party executive, 1936–49; Chairman of Party, 1945–6; author of numerous books including *The American Presidency* (1940), *The American Democracy* (1949). Visited U.S. very frequently.

LEE, HENRY WILLIAM (1865–1932), Sec. of S.D.F., 1885–1911; of B.S.P., 1911–13; Editor of *Justice*, 1913–24; member of International Department of T.U.C., 1926–32.

LEE, JENNIE (b. 1904), daughter of a Fifeshire miner, ed. Edinburgh Univ.; married Aneurin Bevan, 1934; Labour M.P., 1929–31 and since 1945; Director of *Tribune*. Visited U.S. 1932, 1933, 1934, 1935, 1937.

LLOYD GEORGE, DAVID (1863–1945), solicitor in North Wales; Liberal M.P., 1890–1945; President of Board of Trade, 1905–8; Chancellor of Exchequer, 1908–15; Minister of Munitions, 1915–16; Secretary for War, 1916; Prime Minister, 1916–22; cr. Earl, 1945. Author of British "New Deal" proposals, 1935. Visited U.S. 1923.

MACDONALD, JAMES RAMSAY (1866–1937), journalist and politician; joined I.L.P., 1894; Sec. of L.R.C. (later, Labour Party), 1900–11; Treasurer, 1912–24; Labour M.P., 1906–18 and 1922–31; National Labour M.P., 1931–7; Prime Minister, 1924 and 1929–35; Lord President of the Council, 1935–7. Visited U.S. 1897, 1929, 1933.

MANN, TOM (1856–1941), journeyman engineer; Socialist from 1885; leader of London dock strike, 1889; Sec. I.L.P., 1894–8; founder of Workers' Union, 1898; in Australasia, 1901–10; leader of syndicalist movement and (from 1921) member of Communist Party. Visited U.S. 1883, 1913.

M*

GENERAL INDEX